Essential
LIFE SKILLS
for TEENS

Five Dynamic Principles Every Teen and Young Adult
Must Know and Practice to Be Confident, Happy, and
Successful in Relationships, School, and Life

BERNADETTE GREGGORY

Cataloging-in-Publication data for this book is available from the Library of Congress.

DEDICATION

To all the young people in the world who have inspired me and continue to inspire me every day with your wonderful talent, inside-out beauty, incredible ideas, warmth, and goodness. Only you can give your special gifts to the world. Use your gifts to create a world we will all be proud of, now and for always. You can do it!

And to parents everywhere who stand up for your teens and adolescents and support them with compassion and unconditional love as they learn and grow on their journey into adulthood. Don't forget that it's your journey, too, and one you will both remember for the rest of your lives. Make it beautiful.

TABLE OF CONTENTS

INTRODUCTION

What if?

What if you knew what to do when you were given a task you'd never done before?

What if you were able to talk and laugh and feel happy at school and know that when you got home, you could still feel that way? No confrontations, arguments, complaints about how you didn't take out the trash like you were supposed to, and no threats to ground you or take away your phone? What if when you walked through the door, you were met by smiles, positive energy, and unconditional love?

How would you feel if you could be okay with who you are and not worry about bullies, anxiety, or feeling like you'll never belong anywhere? A world where you were worthy just as you are? No need to constantly change to fit in? No need to adapt to the situation but allow it to adjust to you? A world where you are comfortable in your own skin?

What if there were no labels like "depression," "anxiety," or "low self-esteem" to make you feel like you always had to explain your behavior, or take medication when you didn't even know how or why you were feeling or acting that way? What if you could express your feelings and emotions honestly, be safe from judgment and the fear of backlash, and know that you were being listened to and heard? Who would you be without labels? Someone with a beautiful smile, a great sense of humor, a hard worker, a young person capable of doing anything you set your mind to? Who knows how far you could go in life if you could peel away that label and just be who you are? Once you figured it out, of course.

What if you could wake up every single day feeling light and confident that you could face whatever challenge you might face during the day? What if, instead of dreading getting up in the morning, you woke up full of energy and spunk, ready to tackle the world? What if you could believe that at least some of the people you would meet that day are on your side, in your corner, trying to help make your life a little easier? And what if they believed in you so much that you just knew you would find your purpose in life?

And what if that purpose, your reason for being here in this crazy world, turned out to be doing something that you absolutely loved and always dreamed of? Wouldn't that be worth getting out of bed for?

What if?

PARENTS

The teenage years are probably the toughest in the period of life called adolescence. They encompass a myriad of challenges and can be highly stressful for both parents and teens.

Most teens hear "no" more often than they hear "yes," and yet, they are expected to be positive, upbeat, and "perfect," according to the standards of others. After all, what could teens possibly be stressed about? What indeed?

Well, how about their need for belonging, feeling safe to express their emotions, school, which is a full-time job for teens, and being loved no matter what?

Teens don't want to feel helpless or incompetent or that their parents have no faith in them. They need the opportunity to learn and grow. If we don't give them opportunities to show they can be responsible, then how are they supposed to learn these skills and habits?

They don't want to be ridiculed or mocked, for whatever reason, treated like children while being expected to act like adults or punished harshly for something they simply forgot to do. Who would? Nobody I know. What gives them the will and the persistence to get up and try again? The short answer is unconditional love, acceptance, faith, and trust.

Teenagers need to feel that there is always someone in their corner, and sometimes they need help figuring things out. It is our job, as their parents, to be that constant source of support. Reassure them that you are there for them. Look them in the eye and say it out loud, so they know you mean it. "I am here for you. You can come to me with anything, and I will not judge you." Now, this doesn't mean there will not be consequences for their actions, but in that moment, what teens need most is for you to listen without judging. Really listen, and hear them. They need to trust you. They are telling you, in the best way they know how, what they need. If you listen with your heart, you will know what action to take, even if it is just a hug.

Parents often cannot relate to their teens' daily challenges because their own teenage experiences were different from theirs. This makes it hard to communicate because their perspectives are different. How can you work together as a team so you can both get what you want and need? Put yourself in their shoes and understand that these challenges can be overwhelming and even devastating to them. After all, they are still young, and many of these experiences are first-time occurrences. That's one of the reasons they don't know how to handle them. If your efforts to help are insincere, your teen will pick up on that. It usually works out better if you just listen to them. Give them your full attention, so you don't miss anything. While they are talking, they are in the moment. Be in that moment with them so you will know how to respond when the time comes.

Both teens and parents have times when they feel completely helpless, and neither feels empowered to change the situation. Both feel unappreciated, so the stress builds as the silence sends a powerful message neither intends to send.

Then, when the big problems show up—drugs, bullying, depression, feelings of worthlessness and hopelessness, and even thoughts of suicide—you are so crippled with fear that you do nothing. You can't find your way back to each other.

But it doesn't have to be that way.

ADOLESCENTS/TEENS/PARENTS

You have everything you need right now to have a great life. You just don't know it yet, because you haven't lived long enough to see it. But don't stop believing. You'll get there. That inner strength and guidance will show up at just the right time, when you least expect it, and exactly when you need it. So, pay attention.

Work on those communication skills. We'll talk more about that later. You will get better at relationships and take on more responsibility. With that responsibility will come more freedom. The skills you learn here will give you what you need to take your life, regardless of age, to the next level. But it won't happen overnight. Be patient and persistent. Don't give up, and don't listen to people who tell you to.

Once you know what to do and how to do it, you will have the tools to create the life you want. Even if other things you have tried didn't work out for you, you can achieve outcomes you didn't even know were possible. Stick with it. I believe in you. Believe in yourself.

You might even get to see one or two impossible dreams come true. But most of all, you can learn how to live a life filled with joy and happiness.

It might sound like a lot of nonsense, but it isn't. If you can think outside the "enclosure" and consider, for a moment, the "what ifs" in your life, I challenge you to read on and learn how to take the next step. If you can imagine even a small part of the life you want to live—one dream that might come true—then keep reading.

First, you will learn some fundamental life skills. If you are already comfortable with the basics, skip to the next chapter and learn about your emotions and how they work. You'll know how to respond instead of reacting in emotionally charged situations. You'll learn how to read your feelings and understand your brain's role in them.

If you are still looking for your reason for being here on planet Earth and what you can do to make it a better place, I will teach you old and new ways to reach out and help as only you can. You will discover how to tap into your inner self and become your best self.

You'll learn to get through the day without worrying about anxiety or panic. I know this may sound unbelievable to some of you, and it is pretty impressive, but it happens every day for so many young people. So why shouldn't you be one of them?

I will show you how to determine what is most important to you so you can set priorities and boundaries and achieve your goals. Once you learn this valuable skill, you will be able to use it repeatedly throughout your life.

Think of how much more fun your life will be without all those things that drag you down and cause you anxiety and grief. You can use that energy to make everything in your life better.

Family is the most important thing in the world for children of all ages. When raising my daughter, I knew nothing about parenting, which is crazy considering there were twelve kids in my family. I was still a teenager when I moved out of my parents' house to make more room for more kids. We didn't have a lot of money, but we ate well, had clean clothes, and went to church every Sunday. Mama was always there for me, except maybe for the day she made me braid my own hair for school pictures. I still cringe when I look at the picture. Love was the most important thing I learned from my mother. It was never in short supply.

When it was just my daughter and me, it was hard, especially for her. This was because I mostly had only books to learn from, and some of the advice just didn't feel right. Other children with two parents did okay. Their parents seemed to get it right, but I screwed up a lot of the time. I often made decisions without realizing how they would affect my child.

I know you've heard that the teen years are the most important time of your life. As I remember, they weren't so hot. But it all depends on your circumstances. I have learned that teenagers—all children, actually—should be cherished and respected because however good or not-so-good the teen years can be, they are short.

When I raised my child, I didn't understand that even single parents must put their whole hearts into the process. That means to forget about your job, stand up to your boss, who makes you work all the late hours because "you don't have a family," suck it up for eighteen years, and recognize that your top priority is raising your child. If you want a real family, you must put the kids first. They will return your love and acceptance tenfold.

After my daughter grew up and moved out on her own, I took parenting and childcare classes, worked with childcare professionals, and then got into the business myself. I saw how much better life could have been for us, and I wished I'd had a book that told me what to do when I was a teenager.

So, I wrote this one. Maybe it will help you get through some of the best and most challenging years of your life without being ruled by fear, anxiety, depression, and all those other confusing feelings. Teens need an authority figure they can trust to guide them when they can't figure it out themselves. But, if you don't have someone like that, you can practice the skills you'll learn here to help you build a foundation and see where the adventure takes you.

I wish I had known better or more then, but I didn't. That's just the way it was. Now that I know better, I must step up and share the information. There is a way for teens to have an excellent, fun, and happy life without getting caught up in all the modern traps that can lead them down a path from which they may not be able to return. You have a chance to explore new roads. You may have to take a detour from time to time, but I will offer ways to help you get to where you want to be. This book is for you if you are willing to open your mind and heart to new possibilities.

You may notice that I sometimes use the terms "adolescent" and "teen" interchangeably. Adolescence refers to the transitional period when a child grows into an adult. It includes the teenage years, and spans the time of life between the ages of 10 to 19.

Whether you call yourself a teen, an adolescent, or simply the most terrific human being on the planet, which you are, this book is for you. In addition, there are sections directed to parents and others to adolescents and teens. Each is marked so that you can find it easily.

So, are you ready for an adventure? Grab your gear! And keep reading. Remember, we're starting with the basics, so hang in there. Enjoy the book!

CHAPTER 1:
BASIC LIFE SKILLS FOR TEENS

Do not do for your children what they can do for themselves.
–Ann Landers

PARENTS

Parenting a teen can be compared to working at NASA some days. You study for years, land an important job, input all the data, and the screens go blank. Nothing adds up as it should. You wonder how it all went wrong. You have read parenting books and scoured the latest teen blogs, but you still need help.

It may be time to approach this in an entirely new way. You brought home an utterly defenseless human when you first became a parent. It was your job to feed and nurture this little person to help your baby thrive. Throughout the different phases, you taught your new baby how to eat, walk, and even use the toilet, all of the basic survival skills.

Now that you have transitioned to the teen level, it is time to pivot. I understand how difficult this is. You have done everything for this little being since birth, but now it's time to move into the next phase.

This chapter will explore how to begin allowing your teen to become their own unique and independent being while teaching them essential life skills. It may not be easy for parents, but it is necessary for teens.

Plenty of basic skills are available to learn, but you must decide which ones are relevant to your teen and their journey. Mapping out which skills your teen needs to learn and at what age is vital. Often, a teen can feel overwhelmed or even stupid because they don't know how to make a meal or ride the bus. They can hear conversations with their friends who have these skills, and they can feel embarrassed or inadequate. They may not come home and tell you how they felt when they found out a friend knows how to use the city bus system when they've never even been on a bus. On the other hand, they might stand out in class when most know how to measure ingredients and turn on the stove when they group up to make cookies in home economics class. We must be mindful of how much our teens can learn and consider if we are holding them back.

Be sure to sit down and have a conversation with your teen. You may be all set to go with a list of basic needs they need to learn, but have you asked them what they want? They may have a list of things you have not thought about that interest them. Giving them the voice to express their own opinion here is vital.

We want to be sure that we start slowly here. A few things could happen if you sit down with your teenager with an extensive list of new things you want them to learn. First, they may shut down completely. It is pretty common for this to occur when anyone feels overwhelmed. Even if you only have a few things down on paper, this is a great time to talk to them about their ideas. You can always add to that list when you are comfortable.

Second, you may face a situation where your teen refuses to do any of it. When you walk up to a ten-foot-high brick wall, you will often turn your back on it and find another route. Instead, it is best to start slowly. Present them with one or two skills at first, and it is even better to include them in choosing which ones they are. Let them get excited about choosing a new task to learn. Let's face it; we all have some memory of our parents throwing a lawn mower at us in the blazing heat for that first lesson in responsibility. Or insisting we show how responsible we can be by having us babysit our siblings and the neighbors' kids all afternoon while we fear for our lives. Neither of these situations excited us or gave us a passion for lawn care or becoming a parent.

While they begin this new journey, you want to check in on your praise game. Encouragement can go a very long way here. If learning to cook is a new skill they are tackling, you will eat that delicious half-burnt grilled cheese sandwich with a smile, gushing over how delicious it is. Don't get me wrong. You don't want to appear fake. But, if you do, they will know. A gentle bit of advice to lower the heat won't hurt, but be sure to eat that entire sandwich. If you were to refuse to eat it and tell them they failed, they would be devastated and may become an adult who doesn't know how to cook. We have all been here as adults. We pull up a new recipe and get all excited to try it. Anxious with anticipation, we pull it all together. We watch the faces of those we lovingly offer it to taste. Our hearts sink if their faces recoil, and they tell us that it is anything but amazing. We can immediately feel like we never want to cook again. Always be sure to start with a positive comment. "Oh wow, yum! And you managed to get all the cheese to melt." Then you can follow up with constructive criticism. "If you want a trick to avoid burnt edges, just keep that heat on medium, and you will never have to worry, but this is delicious!"

Lastly, if the task is a disaster, try to see it as a great teaching moment, and don't judge. Regroup and discuss the effort they put into it. A small life lesson here can produce excellent results. How often do we put forth a vast amount of effort only to be disappointed with the result, especially the first time we try something? Despite the outcome, we can be proud of the hard work we invested. It speaks to our character. Not giving up, taking a breath, and then giving it another try says so much about who we are as people. The bottom line is our effort can say more about us than the end product. And what an excellent opportunity to give an example of something similar that happened to you. Be sure to keep it light and cheerful, something you can both laugh about afterward. Share the lesson you learned from your experience, even if it was a colossal flop, but don't overdo it. Then talk about the "next time" or change the subject. Let that be your teen's decision. And clean up later.

IMPORTANT LIFE SKILLS YOU CAN LEARN EARLY ON
ADOLESCENTS/TEENS

Throughout this book, I will encourage you to explore the options you have available at your disposal. You have so many choices, but you probably don't know about most of them yet. So please use your beautiful, brilliant brain to find answers to questions beyond what you read here. This is your life, an incredible journey through experiences that will bring you joy and sorrow, pain and healing, and knowledge and wisdom. Some experiences will make you wish you could disappear, and others will make you want to tell the whole world about your accomplishments.

Sometimes it will feel wonderful to know that you don't have to be responsible for earning a living, paying the bills, or worrying about having food to eat. You can curl up in a comfortable chair in your parents' home and let the world go by. Of course, that won't last forever, but you can have the best of both worlds for now. That is, if you are willing to learn to be responsible for doing things you will have to do when you are no longer living with your parents.

Independence is something you have to work for, and it requires responsibility. There is good news, though. You can develop an inner rhythm that will make those responsible routines second nature by doing some things for yourself while you still live at home. Once you do something enough that it becomes a habit, you can do that thing with minimal effort because it will become a part of you. Then, one by one, you can master the skills you need to help you live the life you want.

There is no need to feel overwhelmed and anxious all of the time by reaching for everything at once. You have plenty of time to do the things that are important to you. Take it one step at a time, one day at a time. Experience turns into wisdom once enough time passes that you get to put what you learn into action. Choose your actions wisely, and if you mess up, take a deep breath, step back, and choose again.

MANNERS – WHAT ARE THEY AND WHY ARE THEY SO IMPORTANT?

There is no actual definition for "manners" in most dictionaries, except that it is the plural of "manner." Not much to go on. A manner is a way, maybe even an art, of doing something. I would even go so far as to say that "having good manners" is a way of saying someone took the time to do it right and do it well.

From how you present yourself, to how you use a knife and fork when you eat, to the uncommon kindnesses you offer to people who need assistance – ask them first—you are said to be practicing good manners.

Etiquette is the accepted or dictated way civilized people are "supposed" to behave. There are excellent books on etiquette for which the dictionary does provide a definition.

Oxford Languages, the world's leading dictionary publisher, and Google define etiquette as "the customary code of polite behavior in society or among members of a particular profession or group." Merriam-Webster says it is "the conduct or procedure required by good breeding or prescribed by authority to be observed in social or official life."

"Emily Post's Etiquette," first published in 1922, has stood the test of time. It serves to enlighten all about proper etiquette, otherwise known as good manners. There are also books on business etiquette, but you can work on that later. If you can learn and practice even a few of the basics Ms. Post outlines in her book, anyone will consider you a class act. Your peers would criticize you, of course, but it would only be out of jealousy or feelings of inferiority. Consider the source. If you want to be successful, you need to wear who you are well.

Having said that, let's talk about those of us who are regular people but aren't afraid or embarrassed to be kind, thoughtful, well-groomed, and happy.

But first, let's be real. We are not all raised in the same home or with the same standards and household practices. If you did not learn basic table manners when you were young, this is something you need to start learning now. I am not talking about which fork to use at a fancy dinner, although this skill will come in handy as you get older. In the meantime, you can use this simple tip: Use the utensils one by one from the outside-in.

It's unfair to expect you to know how to use your eating utensils properly when most of what you have eaten in your life has not required them. For example, pizza, hamburgers, hot dogs, fried chicken, ribs, french fries, sandwiches, fruit, ice cream cones, and many other foods do not require a knife, fork, or spoon. Keep that in mind when you are learning and practicing new eating skills.

Here are a few simple things you can practice now.

Don't talk with your mouth full. It is a courtesy to your companions and yourself and can spare you some embarrassment.

Take your time eating to enjoy the food and fellowship, and allow your food to digest properly.

When sharing a meal with others, politely ask if you would like something outside your reach. "Please pass the salt," for instance. Asking "please" and saying "thank you" are basic courtesies. They are also a sign of respect and will usually be appreciated by your dinner companions.

There are other times when saying "please" and "thank you" is appreciated, such as holding doors open for people. If someone goes out of their way for you, send a thank you note or e-mail, or do something nice for them when the opportunity arises. The thoughtfulness of sending a thank you e-mail or phone call will bode well for you in life. If you have their address, a handwritten note will be seen as an uncommon gesture, whether it is a personal or business situation. That simple, handwritten note will stand out among any electronic communication since such thoughtfulness is so rare nowadays.

And remember to shake hands when you greet someone.

These kinds of courtesies present you as a well-rounded individual and help during job interviews and any social situation. The bottom line is to be respectful and use those manners because it will change how others view you and how you see yourself. You might even start a trend among your peers.

It's nonsense to think that young people of today have no manners. It is simply not true. But we are talking about a learned skill here. Whether you learn about etiquette and good manners online, read about proper behavior in a book, or learn simply by watching someone whose behavior you would like to emulate, be up to the task. This is no time to be proud or defensive. Learning this kind of social behavior can be uncomfortable at first, but it can change your life.

The older generations sometimes get hung up on traditional styles of manners, but being a decent human is appreciated at any age. Besides, you can break a few rules. For instance, I wear white whenever I feel like it. I love the color, especially when I am sporting a great tan. I know others who would not dare to break the "no wearing white after Labor Day" rule, but I am definitely not one of them.

COOKING YOUR FIRST MEAL

Knowing how to feed yourself is pretty important. I don't want to see you living on a steady diet of peanut butter and jelly sandwiches when you move out on your own, although nutritionally speaking, you could do worse.

We don't need to be fancy here, but having three to five basic dishes you can make is vital. It's also very impressive.

The poor nutritional value and high cost of take-out food is more than enough reason to learn these cooking skills. I would suggest a pasta dish, a simple meat and potato dish, and a chili or stew that stretches a few meals. You can take this a step further by exploring the grocery store, familiarizing yourself with the aisles, and knowing where to find the ingredients for the dishes you learn to make. Here is a popular recipe to start you off.

Easy Macaroni and Cheese

I chose this one because you can make it all in one pan on the stove, and you don't have to bake it!

Ingredients:

- 5 cups of 2% milk
- 4 ounces cream cheese
- 1 pound white cheddar cheese grated
- 5 tablespoons unsalted butter
- 5 tablespoons flour
- 1 pound dried pasta (macaroni shells)
- 1/2 teaspoon salt
- 1/2 teaspoon pepper

Directions:

1. Find a good size pot and fill it with water, leaving about ten inches from the top, so you have room to add the pasta and allow room for it to boil. Place the pot on a burner and turn the dial to between medium and high. If the pan boils over, don't worry. Just turn the heat down a bit.
2. When the water starts to boil, add a bit of salt to the water and add your pasta. Be careful when adding the pasta, so you don't splash the boiling water on your skin. Cook for about 8 to 10 minutes, but take one shell out and taste it to check so you don't overcook or undercook it.
3. While the pasta is cooking, you can start on your cheese sauce. You will need another good size pot. Melt the butter in it with your burner on low to medium heat. Watch the butter because if the pan is too hot, the butter will turn

brown and ruin the mixture. Now, sprinkle the flour into the butter, whisking together for about two minutes.

4. Next, slowly pour in the milk and continue to whisk. Continue to whisk until the mixture thickens.

5. Turn the heat to low once it has thickened and add your cheddar and cream cheese. Continue to stir and add in your salt and pepper.

6. Add in the cooked pasta. Give it all a good stir, cover with a lid and let it sit for ten minutes.

7. Take off the lid, give a final stir and enjoy!

And voilà, you have completely made your first meal with six basic ingredients.

Any leftovers you have can be placed in a glass or plastic container with a lid and kept in the refrigerator for two to three days or in the freezer for two weeks.

When it comes to food safety, always do your research on how long it is safe to store leftovers. That pizza that has been lingering in your fridge can make you mighty ill if it has been there too long. If you have leftover pizza, freeze it.

ADOLESCENTS/TEENS

Besides the things we've just talked about that will prepare you for life out there on your own, there are some really basic life skills you need to get comfortable with as soon as possible, if you aren't already. They are super simple and super important.

HOW TO DO YOUR LAUNDRY

Doing the laundry looks pretty easy until you have to do it yourself. You know how it is with first-times, though. Looks can be deceiving.

Doing laundry effectively takes skill. Some things you can throw in altogether and some things you can't. Even if your mother or roommate offers to put some of your clothes in with a load of wash they're doing, you still need to contribute to the task. If you have something you really love, you'll want to be more careful with it. It might even be something you want to wash out by hand. If you have it all bundled up in your sheets when you take your Mom or roommate up on their offer, you might not like the outcome.

If you bought something that needs to be hand-washed or dry cleaned, get it out of the laundry hamper before it's too late. If you buy something with your own money, you will probably be more conscientious when it comes to keeping it looking fresh and clean. Clothing that is washable, keeps its shape and doesn't require ironing, is probably the best way to keep it simple. But don't let that stop you from buying something you love. There are care instructions on the label. If you follow them, you should be fine.

I love to iron. I love the feel of cotton and the way clothes look so crisp and clean without wrinkles. I used to do most of the ironing in my family. I didn't even realize it was a chore. It never felt like it to me. But even now, while I still iron, most of the people I know will not buy anything that requires ironing or dry cleaning. If you want to learn this skill, you will probably have to learn it from an older person.

Here's what I recommend for laundry newbies:

Make yourself three piles of clothes—whites, darks, and bright colors. You can keep towels and bedding separate if you want. Washing like materials and colors together keeps your clothes from accidentally transferring the color onto other clothes and keeps clothes looking newer longer. If you just spent a crazy amount of money on that turquoise hoodie and you toss it in with your white t-shirts and your pale pink work shirts, you are going to open that washing machine to a surprise. Bright colors always run the risk of running into other colors. Your whites and work shirt may be blue, and that is permanent. For the first few washes, keep that hoodie in with your jeans and dark colors. As an added precaution, use cold water.

If you are using your family's laundry machines, you have more control over your laundry. Ask your parents to show you what to do. They may have to tell you more than once but don't be discouraged. You can write down the steps so it will be easier the next time, but their input and tips will be very helpful in the long run.

When laundromats are used, there can be leftover bleach and other harsh chemicals left by the previous user. Be careful to choose a machine that doesn't smell like bleach. Follow the directions on the machine or, if there is an attendant, you might get them to help you.

I want to add an important note here. Wash your bedding regularly. Read that again for me. Pick one day of the week that isn't as busy as the other days and make that your bedding laundry day. You don't have to do all your laundry at once, but bedding needs to be laundered weekly. Why? Dead skin cells and sweat build up on your bedding, and so does dust. Dirty sheets can stink up your whole room. It's really gross, but your friends may be too nice to tell you. Clean sheets improve your overall sleep, too. If you have a backup set of sheets, it will make this task a lot easier.

You will learn more about laundry as you get older and more experienced but, for now, this should be enough information to get you started.

LOOKING YOUR BEST

You never get a second chance to make a first impression. You have gone from a kid who loved bubble baths and rubber bath toys to a full-grown adult in a rather short period of time. Parents educate themselves thoroughly on proper hygiene routines for infants, but as teens begin invading the home, they can drop the ball. It is important that you, as a teenager, are aware of your body's changing needs.

The hormones raging through you will alter your personal hygiene requirements. You should be showering daily to prevent acne breakouts and keep your body healthy. And you'll need to invest in a good deodorant. Take some time to research shampoo products for your hair type. There are products for every hair care need.

For older teens, if you have decided to let your facial hair grow, research how to clean and maintain it properly. What razor works best for you, electric or manual? Look at the different costs associated with both of these options as well.

Body washes come in all sorts of scents or unscented, and if you have acne-prone or sensitive skin, you will want to choose accordingly. I always like to adopt a head-to-toe ideal here. Do a checklist daily. What do your hair and scalp need? Did you wash your face and/or treat your beard? Make it a habit as soon as you can. You're not going to want to have to think about it every day. You have more important things to do.

Healthy teeth and good oral hygiene will help you avoid massive dental woes throughout your life. Brush, floss, and visit your dentist regularly. A great smile and fresh breath will be appreciated by both you and the person you're with.

Is your deodorant working or do you need something else? There are many brands and types of deodorants, even aluminum-free deodorants.

Make a list to help you develop a head-to-toe routine that you can refer to daily until your hygiene habits are flawless. That takes around 28 days, or so I've heard. Then, you can go on autopilot and focus on those more important things.

Body wash, a razor, a loofah exfoliating sponge, toothpaste, shampoo, deodorant, and nail care accessories should be on that list. Keep your fingernails and toenails trimmed. If you do a head-to-toe check each day every morning, you should be in good shape.

A friend of mine shared a story recently of her teen son asking why his shampoo bottle still had dancing farm animals on it. We never like to see our babies grow up, so you may have to vocalize your needs.

Your Mom might continue to buy you bubblegum-flavored toothpaste and tearless shampoo well into your thirties, a definite sign that it's time to get your own place. Prolonged adolescence, otherwise known as living in your parents' basement, is not all it's cracked up to be.

CLEANING AND BEING ORGANIZED

If you learn some basic organizational skills now, it will save you some serious grief and time in the future. If you get in the habit of making your bed as soon as you get out of it each day, it will be a game changer. At this stage of your life, it may seem like a huge inconvenience. A messy bed makes a room look immediately disorganized. Your eye is drawn to the massive heap in the middle of the room. When you are feeling exhausted and can't wait to get back to bed, a freshly made bed is so much more inviting. Also, when you are faced with cleaning an entire bedroom, it can seem less overwhelming if you enter the room and the bed is nicely made.

As an adult living on your own, nothing makes you panic more than when someone drops by unexpectedly. You can have a sink full of dishes or be lounging in your pajamas with a Cheeto stuck in your hair. For some reason, visitors always have to pass your bedroom to use the bathroom. If they see a well-made bed, it will actually make you feel better. By the time they emerge from the bathroom, you can have the rest of your house or apartment picked up.

There is nothing more frustrating than when you can't find that book you need, or the sweater you borrowed from a friend, or the elusive car keys. How often do you yell for your Mom because you can't find your bag, phone, hairbrush, water bottle, and so on?

One thing that helps me save time when I am in a hurry is a catch-all bowl just inside my front door. As soon as I walk in, I toss my keys, sunglasses, and anything else I have in my hands, right into that bowl. That way, when I am headed back out, I can grab them, knowing exactly where I left them. You will thank me for this when you are in your own place and you can't lean on your parents to find your missing things in a hurry. It's harder when you're still living at home, sharing space. You can always put that special bowl by the door in your bedroom.

LEARNING THE IMPORTANCE OF MONEY
PARENTS

While some of us were raised in homes that included their young adults in financial conversations, many parents do not talk about finances because they feel these are worrisome adult topics, and shielding their children from them is in their best interest.

This is unfortunate and leads to issues you probably didn't think of. Teens are old enough to learn about money. Not teaching your teens the value of money is a mistake. They may not understand how many hours you need to work to purchase those new shoes for them or to have them on your cell phone family plan. If they understand how household finances work, it gives them an appreciation for both work ethic and the value of money.

One of the best ways for young people to learn about the value of money is to start earning some of their own. Few things are more rewarding than feeling you are contributing something to society and your household and getting paid for it.

Older teens also need to understand credit, but that's a discussion for another day. Start off with the basics. You will be surprised at how much your teens will learn on their own once you give them a little kickstart.

If, by the time they are ready to leave home, your teens have a grasp of basic finances, are able to feed themselves, and can communicate with future professors, employers, and the general public in courteous and mannerly fashion, you will have helped set them on a path to success.

STAYING ACTIVE & HEALTHY
TEENS/PARENTS

Staying active is a sound strategy for a better life. The human body was meant to move, not sit in front of a screen, big or small, all day long, watching other people enjoying their lives. Being active will keep you young at heart as well as in body. Exercise is important, I know, but being healthy takes more than exercise.

When I was younger, nobody's parents ever said, "Do your homework so you can go out and exercise." We didn't exercise. We played. We had fun. We expressed joy. We rode bikes, played catch, went fishing, climbed trees, did handsprings, jumped rope, went for walks with our friends, studied together, played sports, worked in the garden, danced, and laughed out loud at things we thought were funny. Sometimes we just made it up as we went along and waited to tell our parents about our adventures until after we moved out of the house years later.

There are many things we are told not to say nowadays because it might hurt someone else's feelings. But I tend to speak my mind when it comes to being healthy. Obesity is unhealthy. This is not a judgment. It is a fact. It shortens your life and chips away at your mental health. You must learn to see yourself as a whole person, not just a collection of body parts.

Blow off the criticism about your body. If that's all your friends can see, then find new friends. And stop posting things that people can criticize. You don't need their approval and it's none of their business, anyway. Your health is *your* business. Health is about the whole person, body, mind, and spirit. When each of these parts is properly nourished, there is a balance. We feel good, calm, and un-threatened by people and situations around us.

We may eat when our body really wants more sleep. We might continue eating because we do not feel satisfied. But sometimes it's the heart, not the stomach, that is feeling empty. Food is just easier to get than love sometimes. Maybe we need to feel loved and comforted. A hug or having a good laugh with a friend can fill that empty space and the hunger might disappear altogether. It is important to recognize what you really need, what it is that is making you over-eat. Once you figure that out, usually with the help of someone else, you can start working on solving the real problem.

It will take some self-discipline and persistence. Your body didn't get overweight overnight and it will take some work if you want to get back to a healthy weight. Don't give up, and remember, you are beautiful inside and out. You need to know that and be okay with being enough. Love yourself the way you are now and you will eventually grow into the person you always dreamed of being but didn't know that you are already perfect just the way you are. Just don't give up.

There is not one negative thing that can come from being active. It is great for mental and physical health. If you find yourself feeling anxious, go outside and play. Put some music on and go for a walk or run. Any movement at all floods your body with all those feel-good hormones like dopamine and oxytocin, which counteract that anxiety. Having a routine of keeping the body in motion will imprint on your brain, and whenever you are feeling anxious or depressed in the future, it will nudge you to move because it remembers how it felt the last time you did it. It's also great for your heart, your blood sugar levels, and your peace of mind.

Now, you know that going outside is not the only thing that keeps you healthy. You also need to eat things that give your body energy, and stay away from sugar, fats, and junk food that will give you skin conditions, sap your energy and make you fat. You can carry a few extra pounds and still enjoy many activities, but when you are twenty, thirty, and even fifty pounds overweight, your young body is in an unhealthy and dangerous place. It will take more than just eating diet foods, which really aren't good for young people anyway, and pretending being fat is a body image problem, to bring your body into vibrant, radiant health. It can be done, and you don't need anti-obesity drugs or surgery when you are twelve or thirteen years old to fix the problem. Speaking as a former food addict, I know you can do it if you have enough love and support and an eating and exercise program that are right for you. Your healthy weight doesn't have to match the doctor's chart. Everyone's body is different. You deserve to have a healthy life and to enjoy activities that carrying around too much weight can keep you from enjoying. Doing one small thing every day, like not eating anything with sugar in it, can make a tremendous impact on your health. Or you could walk just 15 minutes a day to start seeing results. You have to live in that beautiful body of yours so take care of it. Good health is a lifelong mission. Start now, and watch what happens.

CHAPTER 2:
HERE COME THE EMOTIONS

A self that goes on changing is a self that goes on living.
–Virginia Woolf

PARENTS

Just when you thought you had it all figured out and could sit back and enjoy parenthood for a bit, here come the emotions. We've covered some of the basic life skills your teens need to survive in the outside world, so let's spend some time discussing their developing brains and how this stage of growth and development affects their emotions.

THE FASCINATING ADOLESCENT BRAIN

As parents, we all have vivid memories of teaching our babies to clap their hands, play peek-a-boo, take their first steps, and say their first words. We would jump up and down with excitement, praising them for each accomplishment. When did "Can you say da-da" and "Stand up, walk to Mommy, you can do it" turn into "Sit down and shut up"? Do you remember when you stopped being thrilled with your child's achievements? Maybe you are one of those parents who still proudly celebrates all of their special moments, and if you are, great job! Unfortunately, the majority do not, and it is affecting our adolescents. Your teens still need to know that you are proud of them and their accomplishments and that you support them in their efforts. You could still be hugging them and congratulating them when they bring home great grades or get that first part-time job. You should be oozing with pride when they take on a task like making that first meal all by themselves. I am sure they would appreciate your support when you thank them for trusting you enough to confide in you about something that is important to them.

Teens use a different part of their brain than adults to figure out their emotions. It's called the amygdala. They use their emotions to figure out their emotions. Adults might think with their logical minds but teens tend to think with their feelings. What most of us are unaware of is that adolescents' brains are actually more capable of change than adults. Also, teenagers have the ability to shape their brain development. These amazing beings have hyper-sensitive information processing capabilities, coupled with social sensitivity, to assist them in navigating this new and complex social world they will have to deal with every day.

If we take a closer look at the most recent research on adolescent brain development, we can use this to educate and empower our teens and their parents. This information can help them feel connected to the world around them.

We all know that during adolescence, the body goes through many changes. We do our best to prepare our teens for what is about to come. That being said, what is going on inside that beautiful brain needs to be discussed at length; they need a better understanding of why they are feeling the way they are. As parents, we would benefit from this information as well. Puberty will come and go, but that brain is going to continue to change well into their twenties (Haynes, 2008, p. 273–281)

It is this constant change occurring in the brain that causes so many changes in the behaviors of our teens.

Here are some important facts about grey matter: It holds the majority of the neuronal cell bodies and creates regions of the brain that are vital for self-control, decision-making, sensory perception, and muscle coordination. The grey matter in the adolescent brain actually decreases by 1.5% per year (Haynes, 2008, p. 273–281).

Don't panic. This is actually a good thing. The science community tells us that the decrease in gray matter is in conjunction with the connections being made between brain cells! They are making way for more white matter. Each time the teen makes a decision in his or her everyday life, connections, and neural pathways are formed.

One of the best resources I have found on adolescent brain development is KidsHealth, a joint initiative between The Paediatric Society of New Zealand and Starship Foundation. Their website is https://www.kidshealth.org.nz/adolescent-brain-development.

WHAT'S THE MATTER WITH TEENAGERS TODAY?

PARENTS/ADOLESCENTS/TEENS

You don't have to go far to hear negative talk about the youth of today. "What is wrong with those teenagers today?" "Why would you do something so stupid?" Teenagers have been acting irresponsibly and doing impulsive things for generations. This is not something new. Of course, the older generation would like to believe that the teens of today are worse. The teens of the 1950s were stealing their parents' cars and sneaking off to the drive-in movie. The teens of the 1970s lied to their parents to spend the weekend at Woodstock. Each generation has its version of "troubled teens." My question is, why have we not started educating ourselves on the "why" of these behaviors? Knowledge is power, and especially in the times we face today, it is vital.

I know that most adults, when faced with something that troubles them, try to find out the reason in order to gain a solution. Sarah has an itchy rash, so she visits the doctor and finds out it is an allergy.

She gets some medication and feels better. Jamal is feeling extreme sadness since his best friend died in a motorcycle accident. He goes to see a grief counselor twice a month, and he gets the support he needs to carry on and he starts to feel better.

As our teenagers struggle through normal growth and development changes, hormone fluctuations, new and often confusing emotions, and life circumstances in general, we need to be aware that these things affect them deeply. If we dismiss their feelings and simply bark orders at them like "You need to do better in school" or "You forgot to take out the trash" while acting annoyed that they took us away from our oh-so-urgent text, we cause them unnecessary mental anguish. They have enough going on, and their feelings which, I can assure you, are deeper than most adults realize, are very hurt. This is a hurt that often manifests itself in anger. How quickly we forget how we felt when we were teens.

So, what is it that teenagers actually need? These teenage humans need what we all need at that age. They need unconditional love, understanding, and most importantly, connection. That feeling of connection allows them to learn what they need next on their journey to adulthood.

Connection is a sacred link from our hearts to the Source of all creation. It honors human spirit but acknowledges the needs of human animal. A broken body can be healed more easily than a broken spirit. If you've ever lost that connection to yourself, you know what I mean. More on that in Chapter 6.

THE EMOTIONAL JOURNEY
ADOLESCENTS/TEENS

Please be patient, not only with your parents, but also with yourself. It's been a long time since your parents were teenagers. Help them put themselves in your shoes. Talk to them, and be willing to listen. This may be a tough thing to do, but most adolescents deny or at least resist the changes in their bodies that make them feel like they're not in control. Well, chances are your parents feel that way too. Everyone resists change, at first.

Much of what is happening to you in terms of emotions and feelings is part of the natural process. I don't know why it happens like that, or why it takes so long and is so uncomfortable, but I do know that there are times you have to trust your body. Don't be so quick to label yourself. There is not a quick fix for adolescents and teens who just want to make certain feelings go away. Much of the anxiety and confusion will go away on its own. You will grow out of it. I speak as a parent and someone who is very familiar with child development.

You will not find the answers to all your questions on social media or any other resource that has its own agenda. For those of you who don't know what that means, it basically means that they are telling you to do one thing or another because there's something in it for them. They will profit from your vulnerability, and they will give you whatever information they feel like and hope you will fall for it. I hope you won't.

Communication is vital when emotions are flaring and all those teenage things you can't help doing conspire to get you in all kinds of trouble. One cannot have a quality life without effective communication. And it doesn't happen overnight. It takes some time before our experiences and knowledge merge into wisdom, but they will. The more you practice your communication skills, the more comfortable you will be speaking your mind in a respectful way and asking for what you need.

We must acknowledge that the teenage years are a time of transition and they can be filled with many struggles. Your brain is changing, your body is changing, hormones are flooding you, and most of the time, nobody is explaining any of this. Most days, you must feel as if you went to bed as a child and woke up as an adult. One moment, we place adult expectations on your shoulders with no guidance on how to accomplish them. When you fail, you are often met with harsh criticisms like, "Grow up; you aren't a kid anymore." I mean, how confusing is that? These scenarios may make you start to ask yourself questions like, "Who am I?" or "Why can't I do anything right?" and perhaps the worst one, "Why am I even here?"

Nobody wants to feel that way. It may seem like you have nowhere to turn, but have you given your parents an honest shot? There is a chance they don't know how you feel. As parents, we can drop the ball when it comes to reading our teenagers, but we want you to be healthy and happy. Ask your parents to have a conversation with you and explain the pressure you are feeling. If you feel awkward about a face-to-face conversation, write them an email or letter.

I recommend a letter. That way you can say what you need to say without your emotions getting the better of you. You can read it over a few times and let it sit for a couple of days until any anger you might be feeling has subsided, and you have expressed your true concerns.

Don't get me wrong. I am not saying to sugar-coat it. It's just that once you click "Send", it's too late to take it back. Letters that parents can read away from the distracting screens of their phones or computers force them to be in the present moment. They can hold the letter in their hands and feel your pain. They can read it over and empathize with you in a way that most modern-day hit-and-run conversations don't allow.

Be respectful and do your best to outline your feelings. Tell them if you've been feeling overwhelmed, if you haven't felt heard, and most of all, tell them what you need from them. Give them a chance to help.

If opening up to your parents is not an option, lean on a great friend, another family member, a teacher, or ask your parents about therapy. There are wonderful psychologists who specialize in working with young people. You can talk it out with most issues without the need for medication or radical treatments. Having an unbiased ear to listen to you is so very important in these situations. You want to feel connected and heard. You matter. But some things are just too big to solve on your own. It is brave and courageous of you to reach out and use your voice when you need help.

PARENTS

Establishing positive relationships with friends, family members, or any single person can reduce anxiety and ward off depression. That feeling of being connected to yourself boosts self-esteem. Pay attention. Reach out to your teen. They probably won't make it easy. We didn't. Those first few times of asking, "Are you doing all right?" will likely be met with an answer of, "I'm fine," or "I'm cool" but be persistent. Open-ended questions are better, of course, if your relationship is ready for that. Show them you care. Be a person they can trust. Keep the communication lines open, and keep your phone out of the conversation.

Being there for your teen requires a commitment. Don't make promises you can't keep. They will forgive you the first few times but after that, they will start looking elsewhere for someone they can count on.

The emotional journey is challenging and rewarding, not always at the same time, though. But you *can* do this if you start now. No excuses or justifications. You are not trying to win your teen's approval. You are trying to help them become the best person they can be. You are the person who can help make that happen, so you have work to do. Educate yourself.

You might want to check out this interesting and informative website, for starters. The company is Teen Brain Trust. You can find it at https://teenbraintrust.com/. They have a newsletter, Teen Prompts, that you can subscribe to for $7.99 a month. There are many useful tips and they're all in one place.

Don't stop there, though. Keep researching but leave room for your own thoughts and opinions. This is your adolescent, your teen, and the choices you make affect all things to come. Read, study, and stay informed, but remember, it's your parenting that counts. Don't let others bully you into doing things you don't feel in your heart are right for your teen and for your family.

MANAGING DIFFICULT EMOTIONS
PARENTS/TEENS

Anger
Anger may be the most difficult emotion of all the emotions to manage. Anger is a response to fear. When you think someone has

done something to hurt you on purpose, you may want to strike out at them, curse, mock, or punch them, or something worse. You may feel like you want to get even and hurt them because they hurt you. Later, most people regret actions they took in anger, but some don't. I talk a lot about unconditional love as it is one of the five dynamic principles we will discuss later in the book. And yes, this is a good time to bring it up again.

You are not responsible for the actions of others, and you cannot control what they do. However, you can control what you do and how you respond to their actions. You have the power to change your mind and choose another response instead of reacting to the actions of another.

Some things aren't about you; they're not your fault. It's hard enough to be responsible for yourself growing up, let alone everybody else's issues. Angry people aren't very happy people. They feel bad and they like to make you feel worse, as if that will make them feel better, knowing that you are both miserable. Thus, the phrase, misery loves company. Fear can make you do a lot of things and it's a good idea to stay away from angry people. There are many weapons of anger, and some of them are deadly. One of the deadliest ones is the automobile. Look at road rage. It's a perfect example.

Anger can be good sometimes because it can be a real motivator. It is also the only way some people are able to express negative feelings. They let everything build up and then they explode. Sometimes the person they are lashing out at doesn't even know why.

Hopefully, you will be able to use the techniques in this book to help you get through some of the tougher life experiences teens inevitably face. And if you encourage your teen to keep practicing the skills and principles, you will be able to avoid many frustrating challenges. Anger is like a boomerang. It always comes back to bite you in the backside. There are anger management classes for those who need a little extra help.

Grief

Everyone grieves in their own way. There is very little you can do to console the one who has just endured a great loss, no matter what you say or do. Grief is felt when any loss takes place, not just death. It may be the loss of a loved one, a parent or a close friend, a pet that you could always count on to comfort you when you were feeling down, or a job you loved but lost when the company downsized. It could even be moving away from your home to a new place and leaving behind people and things you loved.

Grief has five stages according to Swiss-American psychiatrist Elisabeth Kübler-Ross. They are denial, anger, bargaining, depression, and acceptance. Grief is sometimes mistaken for depression. Feelings can get all jumbled up and look the same on the outside. Just knowing what you are truly feeling can help you identify the real problem and heal the hurt you are carrying around.

Anxiety

Anxiety is a very popular feeling among teenagers. It has to do with expectations and worrying about what might happen in situations over which you have little or no control. Anxiety takes a lot of energy and rarely affects the outcome of a situation. This is a good time to find a calm space, let your mind rest for a moment, maybe do a meditation, or just do nothing. One thing you can do to alleviate anxiety is to stay in the present moment. Don't worry about things you can't control. You took the test. Your grade will be what it is whether you dwell on it or not. Let the past moment go and calm your mind. Focus on what's happening now and let the rest be what it is.

Depression

There are different stages of depression. You can have the blues but you don't necessarily need to be medicated for feeling down or having a bad day. However, your body will send all its energy to the area that needs it the most when it senses a problem. If the part of you that is hurting takes so much of your energy that you are unable to do the things that are part of your everyday life, you may need a little extra help. There is always a reason we feel the way we do, but we may not always be able to figure it out on our own. Sometimes we just can't snap out of it. Everybody needs a little extra help once in a while. If you are feeling that way, you might want to talk to your guidance counselor, pastor, or Mom and Dad.

When depression becomes so bad that all of your thoughts are dark, it's time to call in reinforcements. There are crisis and suicide hotlines whose staff deal with these issues every day. They can help you find someone to guide you through the darkness and free yourself from the negative hold your feelings have on you.

If you live in the United States, you can dial 988 from any phone to connect with the Suicide and Crisis Hotline, anytime, day or night. These calls are meant to be anonymous.

A word to the wise, though, in case you choose to confide in an authority figure other than your parents, persistent and long-lasting negative thoughts make you very vulnerable. Listen to that little voice inside. Unless your parents are physically, emotionally, or sexually abusing you, taking drugs, leaving you with no food in the house, or some similar behavior, they have a right to know if you are being counseled by a teacher or any other authority figure without their permission. If such an authority figure tells you not to tell your parents, find someone more professional to confide in.

Don't wait until things get so bad that you feel like no life at all is better than the one you have. This is a time to calm your mind and banish those scary thoughts. You may need help doing that. One of the hardest things we face in our lives is recognizing that we cannot do everything ourselves. Sometimes we need to ask for help. No matter how smart you are, how many things you can do, how much money you have, how much you know, how many friends you have, or how many people think you should be able to do it all on your own, sometimes you need help. Ignore the outside noise and listen to that voice within. Be brave and trust yourself. Reach out and get the help you need, and don't stop asking until you get it. Your mind will resist like crazy. It doesn't like things to change. It's too scary. But you need to muster up all the courage you have—and believe me, you have plenty—and make that call. It doesn't mean you are weak. It means you are humble enough to set your ego aside and let something greater take over, get you over the hump so you can have your life back again.

PARENTS

According to the National Alliance on Mental Illness, suicide is the second-leading cause of death for people 15 to 24 years old in the United States. Almost 20% of all high school teens are reported as having had serious thoughts of suicide. Terrifyingly, 9% have made a legitimate attempt on their young lives (Cohen, 2022, par. 1). These are heartbreaking statistics. The suicide rate for this demographic is higher than it has ever been, and it is rising. We need to sit up and take notice before this bleak picture gets any worse.

Reading the statistics on suicide in the teen demographic should alarm anyone. If you think this would never happen to your child, think again. Most adolescents who take their lives are not troubled youth. They are intelligent, capable human beings with bright futures. They became bogged down, stressed out, and not heard. When no one cares what you have to say, your self-worth takes a nose dive. We need to form solid connections with our teens not only because we love them, but to keep them safe.

If you make a solid effort to connect with your teen right now, it will make a huge difference. Be that soft and supportive place for them to land, regardless of what they are going through. Make it known that they can come to you with anything, even those awkward or embarrassing things. And unless it is literally a matter of life and death, keep it confidential. Feeling they have nowhere to turn can lead to a dark place from which they may not be able to return.

Meanwhile, back at Hormone Central, hormones are raging in those young bodies like never before. It's up to us as responsible parents to make sure our teens are getting accurate and reliable information about what's going on in their bodies and how these changes affect them physically, emotionally, and psychologically.

It can be embarrassing to ask your parents questions about puberty or talk about feelings that you have never felt before and don't even understand yourself. There is information all over the Internet and for many teens, their main source of information is social media. Discussions among their peers are also happening, and I don't have to tell you how often your teens listen to their peers instead of their parents.

Many, if not most, of the feelings of confusion and uncertainty teens experience around the time of puberty will vanish after puberty. These feelings are natural, although they can be very uncomfortable. Their brain is growing, their body is changing. Of course, the messages can get confusing. It's like any other life cycle.

There are many reasons for teens to feel uneasy and generally dissatisfied with their lives during this period of transition from childhood to adulthood. Look beyond the labels for reasons for this dissatisfaction. In most cases, it's just the body moving so fast that their minds and emotions can't keep up. Financial pressures in the home, sudden grief or trauma, school pressures, sleep deprivation, loneliness, and even world chaos, can make them feel confused, even hopeless. A good therapist can help with that, and a child psychologist is infinitely more qualified to help your teen work things out in a professional setting.

Dysphoria is a common buzzword now. It is a psychiatric term. When I worked at a psychiatric hospital for children and adolescents, I learned that every psychiatric label is associated with medication and money. That may sound harsh, but it's true. Dysphoria is defined by the Mayo Clinic as "a state of feeling uneasy, unhappy, or unwell". Who hasn't felt that way at one time or another?

Gender dysphoria is another matter altogether. It is a topic you need to discuss with your parents first, not someone who might give you false information based on their own opinion, or make your parents out to be monsters who don't know what they are talking about and don't want to do the right thing for you. This is a serious topic with lots of different information to sort through. Look at all the information and come up with a few questions you and your parents can discuss.

Familiarize yourselves with this subject. Since gender dysphoria is now being presented as the main reason young people have so many issues, you need to get a jump on it. When your vulnerable, underaged child is persuaded—by anyone—to, without your permission, undergo a procedure so radical as to change their body permanently in order to make them feel better about who they are, you have a fight on your hands. If your teen trusts you enough to come to you first, you can talk with them about their feelings and thoughts on the subject. Keep an open mind, but inform yourself with accurate and correct information so you will know what you're talking about when the discussion comes up.

Dr. Miriam Grossman, a child and adolescent psychiatrist, gave a very interesting interview about gender dysphoria and transgenderism on American Thought Leaders on Epoch TV, an online resource I often use for research. It was a two-part interview. Part 1 is titled "How One Doctor's Lies Built the Gender Industry" and Part 2 is titled "The Sexualization of Young Children". Both interviews were enlightening but sometimes difficult to watch. It's that bit about not knowing what you don't know. I highly recommend that you and all parents take the time to learn the truth about this controversial topic so that you can discuss it intelligently with your teens. Out-in-the-open discussions have a way of alleviating the anxiety caused by confusion and doubt.

Epoch TV is a paid subscription but you can pay $1 for a trial period of a month or more that will give you plenty of time to study the video interviews. I encourage you to educate yourself about gender dysphoria and gender-affirming practices before the questions start. Dr. Grossman's interviews are a great place to get the basics, and you can continue your research from there. Here is link that will take you to both interviews: https://www.theepochtimes.com/dr-miriam-grossman-how-one-doctors-lies-built-the-gender-industry-part-1_4852600.html

FEELINGS THAT PLAY A BIG PART IN YOUR LIFE
PARENTS

Fred Rogers, from the highly acclaimed and immensely popular children's program, "Mister Rogers' Neighborhood" was the subject of the 2018 documentary, "Won't You Be My Neighbor?" The documentary film, which was introduced at the Sundance Film Festival and released in the United States later that summer, highlighted Rogers' groundbreaking work with children that began in the late 1960s. Grossing $22 million, it was the largest grossing biographical documentary ever produced. Watching the film reminded me of how much the youth of today miss by clinging so tightly to their phones and forgetting what it is like to have a real friend. The program ran for 33 years, from 1968 to 2001. Television had just begun featuring programming for children when Rogers introduced the program on public television. His dignified and unique approach to teaching children in their early childhood years was embraced by parents and children alike. He was clearly ahead of his time. Rogers received a Lifetime Achievement Emmy for the program in 1997 and was awarded the Presidential Medal of Freedom in 2002. "Won't You Be My Neighbor?" is available on Netflix and other media sources. I encourage you to watch it.

There is a gap between the early childhood years and the adolescent years that can be difficult for parents to recognize. This film shows the importance of understanding how children think and feel as they grow and develop and emphasizes the importance of connection as well as educating parents who are not aware of this approach to early childhood development.

SELF-CONFIDENCE
ADOLESCENTS/TEENS
Adapting to the world of adolescence can leave your self-confidence a bit shaky. You are so busy learning all the time. You are being flooded with information at school, and your brain is being overloaded by screens and your parents' expectations. During this time, you will learn to drive (if you choose to), apply for jobs, and graduate high school, all while growing and changing. Your physical appearance will also change while all of this is going on. It is quite remarkable when you think about it, but it's no wonder your confidence can get a little wobbly.

On the bright side, self-confidence will serve you well in your life. It will help you make really great choices and know, in your gut, that you chose wisely. You won't feel the need for someone to confirm you made the best decision, although it is nice to feel validated. You will stand taller, make informed choices, and look people in the eye when you talk to them.

So, how do you build self-confidence? There are some things you can start doing for yourself to boost your self-confidence a few notches. For instance, do your parents still make most of your decisions for you or do you make them for yourself? If they do, now is the time to start making more on your own. Teenagers can feel uneasy about making their own decisions, especially the first time, but as you start making more of those decisions on a regular basis, you will feel your confidence growing.

We can start small here; for instance, when you are in the car and it needs gas, why don't you jump out and pump it? It might be terrifying those first couple of times, but soon you will feel super confident in that ability. If you are pumping gas for someone else, there is a little gas pump icon on the dashboard with arrows. If the arrow is on the left side of the icon, the gas tank is on the left side of the car. If the arrow is on the right side, the gas tank is on the right.

Once you feel confident in that one skill, choose another one to practice. How about offering to make dinner? This could include a trip to the grocery store to find all of the ingredients. Again, start off small. That first week, you could try the macaroni and cheese recipe included in this book. Maybe the next week, you can push your skills a little further. Just don't over-commit. You still have school or your part-job, and your other daily tasks to consider. Remember, take care of yourself. That's important. You're important.

Another way to build self-confidence is through effective communication. I have no doubt that there are times when you attempt to express your opinion with your parents and it turns into an argument. You may not even get to say what you wanted to say before you storm off in frustration.

Why don't you ask your parents for some practice sessions? This could go either way, so keep an open mind. It could be a lot of fun. Tell them that you want to feel more comfortable communicating with them and ask them to do some role-playing. I'd start with 15-30 minutes for the first session. You can tell them what you have in mind and what you would like to gain from the role plays, and then let them talk. That should give you a few ideas. Try it out and see what happens. If it doesn't work, at least you tried. You can always try something else.

PARENTS

Just as you taught your children to ride a bike and brush their teeth, fostering self-confidence is also part of your role as a parent. Being self-confident will help them make great choices without being influenced by others. We don't want to force them into a sport or hobby we loved when we were younger if it isn't something they are interested in. They may go along because they don't want to let us down but if it's not what they truly want, it could cause resentment. Model self-confidence for them. Be mindful of their mood after a game or practice. Show empathy, but don't discount their feelings either way. Their feelings are important so don't project. Always remember, you are the biggest role model your teen has, so be mindful of your own actions.

Regardless of the situation, be that positive cheerleader. They are going to be hard enough on themselves. We always want to be the ones building them up, not the opposite.

SELF-ESTEEM
ADOLESCENTS/TEENS

Self-esteem is about how you value yourself as a person. It doesn't have anything to do with all the things you can do or the awards you have won, although recognition is one of the things employees say means the most to them. I imagine they're not the only ones who feel that way. People want to be seen and heard. We all want to know we've not been forgotten. This is very important when you're growing up. You need to know that you are loved and valued. The more you value yourself, respect yourself and your needs, the more settled you will feel inside, and the calmer you will be. That inner calm is a special kind of happy.

You know, even the most accomplished adults can struggle with feelings of low self-esteem. That can lead to some pretty tough emotional challenges. Sometimes self-confidence isn't enough to get you through. When the situation calls for more than self-confidence can offer, you need gumption, spunk, courage, or whatever you want to call it. You have to go for it, fearlessly, and see it through. Like Winston Churchill once said, "If you're going through hell, keep going." You just don't want to get stuck there.

A friend of mine, whom I shall call "Fiona", has two sons, one of whom is now an adult. When the older one was fifteen and heading into the tenth grade, they found out he needed glasses and braces in the same month. He also went from being a tiny wee thing to being six feet tall in about three months. And then he broke out with cystic acne. That's a lot for a teenager to take on all at once. I mean, here was this high school kid, just getting to know his changing body, slammed with glasses, braces, horrible acne, and a growth spurt of about two feet in a very short period of time. He felt so defeated; he didn't want to go to school. It is pretty hard to feel great about yourself in those circumstances.

Let's be honest. Your peers can be brutal and unkind, and not just in person. They light up social media with comments that cut through the soul. What can you do? You have to get through it somehow. Lean on the support of family, friends, and anyone you can confide in. You just have to do the best you can and get through it. It might be a good time to ditch social media for a while since it can have quite a negative impact on your self-esteem. Consider the source and let the negative energy go.

Shift your thoughts to your dreams and goals, and things that matter. Those people don't. And there's nothing you can do about the rest right now, so keep going. You cannot control what others do so un-friend them and let them own their own actions.

Fiona's son is 26 years old now. He outgrew the acne, wears contacts now, and has one of the most fantastic smiles you've ever seen. He graduated from the university with a degree in computer science, and he landed his dream job with a big tech company in Germany. They talk about his days of being bullied and how it shaped him as a man. He does not diminish how tough it was at the time. He withdrew a lot during that time, and it made him feel more isolated and lonelier than he needed to feel. But he made it through.

His advice is to stay in contact with your family. The shame he felt might have been avoided. He said it really belonged to those trying to make him feel less than he was. I feel that his advice is sound. Stay close with your family and let them help you when you are going through a rough patch. You will prevail, eventually, if you don't give up, and your self-esteem will be reinforced.

PARENTS

My own experience as a parent wasn't quite like that. I learned, after my daughter was an adult living on her own, what I wish I had known when she was growing up. She gave me so many chances, but I missed most of the signs because I was focused on my own survival and not on what she was going through. Things got better for us from time to time, but we never had the experiences my friend Fiona had, the ones you have together, as a family. My daughter did most everything on her own. Another Winston Churchill quote comes to mind. "It's not enough that we do our best; sometimes we have to do what's required." She always did that. I learned it from her. She moved far away and I didn't get to see her very often, which I have always regretted. She put herself through college waiting tables and doesn't owe a penny in student loans. She achieved so many things that I didn't get to be a part of.

As I watched that documentary on Fred Rogers, I wondered why I didn't know about "Mister Rogers' Neighborhood" when my daughter was young.

If your teens do not feel loved in the way they need to feel loved, unconditionally and without judgment, they will lose their sense of belonging, their sense of family, of community. If you are too busy to listen to them and aren't there when they need you, they will stop asking after a while and look for what they need somewhere else. If they feel that they can never seem to be able to do enough to deserve your love, they will begin to feel unworthy and behave in ways that match those feelings.

Those behaviors can include:

- Engaging in alcohol or drug use
- Overeating
- Avoiding friendships
- Acting out
- Lack of motivation
- Depression

Don't wait until it gets to that point. There is someone just around the corner or down the street waiting to take over your job. Be there for your teens. Be someone they can count on, not just when times get tough but always. It may take some work depending on how solid your relationship is, but there are resources available that can help. Don't be ashamed or afraid to ask, but be careful to choose someone who truly has your child's best interest, and yours, at heart, and will keep you in the picture.

EMPATHY
ADOLESCENTS/TEENS/ PARENTS

In basic terms, empathy is the ability to feel another's pain. It can be a person, a pet, or any living being with feelings, which is almost everything. You can feel it in the words of a song that causes you to break down sobbing for what you feel is no reason at all. You can feel it in the despair or disappointment of someone who has just endured the loss of a friend or parent, or a pet. It's like getting in their skin and feeling what they are feeling. Empathy is different from sympathy when you feel sorry for a person's troubles. This is something deeper and more open. You feel as if it were happening to you.

Parents feel it for their children and vice-versa. Empathy allows you to feel someone's pain and still let them feel it without interrupting their tears or trying to calm them with kind words. People need to let out their feelings in times of crisis, so let them. Open your heart and close your mouth. Let your ears do the rest. Just be there for them if they need you and be gracious enough to leave if they don't.

One of the good things about having empathy is that when you feel the experience that vividly and intuitively, you can often avoid having the same thing happen to you. There usually isn't enough time in one lifetime to have all the experiences we want or need to have. Therefore, having empathy can save you from a world of hurt and heartbreak because you already know how it feels. Besides that, it makes you a better person.

ACCEPTANCE
ADOLESCENTS/TEENS

There is nobody in the world like you. There never was and there never will be. You are uniquely you. You are perfect just the way you are. You are not a mistake. You are the way you are for a reason, which you will find out more about as you get a little older. You don't need to be fixed and you don't need to do anything special to be worthy of love.

It is so hard to accept ourselves the way we are, the way we look, the way we do things, and even the way we love, especially if we are criticized all the time. But, you see, if we can't accept ourselves, how can we expect others to accept us, and how can we accept others? It all starts with us. It starts with us; everything does.

You are beautiful inside and out. It's true that many people look at the wrapping on the human package first before they can decide if what's inside the package is worth unpacking. It's a good thing we don't do that with other things, or we'd have a lot of empty boxes lying around. Think about it. Would you rather be the gift or the wrapping?

When you're a teenager, you want others to like you. You want to have friends to do things with, and you want to feel like you belong somewhere. It's a wonderful feeling to belong. It's a family feeling. It feels safe and warm, and you don't feel scared when you know you're surrounded by people who care about you. When you don't have this, and I know a lot of you don't, your comfort turns into dread and feelings that you are not good enough because if you were, wouldn't they choose you?

You are not the only one who feels that way. Many people do, even grown-ups. And it feels awful.

PARENTS

Who better to accept your teen completely than you? This child of God you brought into the world, this beautiful little being who counted on you for everything, who trusted you no matter what, still does. And now here you are, many years down the road with a few more to go, with your beautiful teen needing just as much love and acceptance as they did then.

It is crucial for your teen to feel accepted for who he or she is. If you want to give them one thing that sends their self-esteem over the moon, remind them of how much you still love them, and remind yourself, too. Stop calling them out on every little thing. Let them grow into the best person they can be. Don't complain about their behavior or compare them to someone else. If you need to talk, talk to them with the same respect you'd show a friend or neighbor. When we complain, our children, young and older, tend to think we are blaming them, which sometimes we are.

How do you show acceptance? You shower them with unconditional love and support. If they go out into this world knowing that they have this support system, they will be willing to try things that lead to establishing their independence. Acceptance doesn't equate with approval. Approval comes from neediness. Acceptance comes from unconditional love.

If your teen comes to you and says they have decided to try a new hairstyle, and your gut is screaming that it is a bad idea, you smile and drive them to the appointment. Allow them to explore new horizons but remember, your first job is to protect them and keep them safe, literally and figuratively, and guide them. It wouldn't be wrong to set some boundaries regarding decisions. I would ask, "What kind of hairstyle were you thinking about?" since not being old enough to drive is in itself a sign that a little guidance might be in order. Each decision your teens make reinforces their own personhood. However, this does not mean that you allow your child to do whatever they want just because that's what "everyone else is doing". You are the parent. Don't forget that. Your teen is your responsibility. You do not answer to your child, your friends, or other people your child has contact with who might have different family values from yours. Stick to your values but be open to what comes next.

FORGIVENESS

"Forgiveness is the fragrance that the violet sheds on the heel that has crushed it."
–Dr. Wayne Dyer

ADOLESCENTS/TEENS/PARENTS

Forgiveness is an emotion-based coping strategy that can be difficult to comprehend for people of all ages. It is a learned skill. Research has shown that it can take many years for some people to grasp the concept of forgiveness. We partly learn this skill from our parents or caregivers. (Enright, 2019)

There will be times in your life when people will hurt you in ways that make you want to fight back but can't for one reason or another. When we carry those hurts inside, going over and over how we will handle it the next time, the hurt goes deeper. The human spirit is very strong but sometimes these deep hurts that we can't seem to let go of cause us to feel broken inside. Forgiveness is a way to let go of the pain and become whole again, so we can move past the hurt and live the life we were meant to live.

Forgiveness, one of the Five Dynamic Principles discussed later in this book, is necessary to clear the path of obstacles we throw in our own way. One of those obstacles is punishing ourselves for something someone else did. More on forgiveness in Chapter 7.

CHAPTER 3:
FINDING YOUR PURPOSE IN LIFE

*There is no greater gift you can give or receive than to honor your
calling. It's why you were born. And how you become most truly alive.*
– Oprah Winfrey

ADOLESCENTS/TEENS/PARENTS

This chapter explores the connection between one's purpose in life and the things they love the most. Intuition is your best guide to finding where you belong in the world.

Lester Levenson who created The Sedona Method, said "Intuition is only right 100% of the time." The laws of the universe are the same for all of us. But understanding our connection to God, Source, Creator, the Great Spirit, or any of the thousands of other names this unseen source of all creation has been called, allows us to tap into a huge energy source that flows through all of us.

There is a presence within each of us that knows and notices. Many problems need creative solutions that the mind cannot provide. It can be very frustrating. But intuition goes beyond the mind, through the heart, and connects to the Source. In this space, there is no fear, only love. Fear is to the mind what love is to the heart. The two never meet in the same place. When you have a problem and you have thought of every possible solution and none of them work, then it's time to go within and get creative!

When you learn to trust your intuition, you are on your way to living a successful and dynamic life.

Who am I and what am I doing here? These are questions that everyone asks themselves at some time during their life. Finding your purpose in life means identifying that special thing that you were put on this earth for. There is a good reason you are here. You have something of value to contribute to family, friends, the world, and the Universe and it's your job to find out what that is. You find it by living your life and paying attention.

We have become a lazy society with many people wanting to get something for nothing. Unfortunately for them, you get out of life what you put into it. If you do nothing, you get nothing. That's just the way things are. The worst part about people who think they are entitled to have whatever they want without contributing anything to society, is that they will never be happy. There will always be anger and hate and judgment in their lives. They will never be satisfied and they will always want more because they have been conditioned to feel "worth-less" than they are. Their "more" will come only when they are ready to accept the fact that they deserve to have goodness in their lives and no one can make that happen except them. It isn't about doing more so you can get more. It is about being more so you are more. Then the things you need have a way of coming to you. You may not always get what you want, but you can always get what you need. When you understand this, you will never have to struggle again. No matter what challenges life may bring, you can rise up to meet them with dignity and honor.

Your purpose finds you when you're ready. It whispers to your heart. The first thing you need to do is to be okay with doing something you love. The thing that makes you happy will bring joy to others, because you will share it with them. Some people don't believe that. They are more focused on money and survival, but there is more to life than just surviving.

Your purpose shows up when you do. What does that mean? What is happening now in your life adventure is what you are ready for. You will learn how to level up, take risks, and go the distance for your dreams. You will have to work for what you want because nothing works unless you do. That's just the way it is. If you want to take your dream to the next level, you will have to make some changes, and probably some sacrifices, too.

Yes, you may have some friends who already know what they want to do but it doesn't happen that way for everybody. As you move along your adolescent journey toward adulthood, you will discover that many successful people change their professions as their interests change or their quest for purpose and meaning intensifies. There is nothing wrong with that. Don't be afraid to change your mind if you feel yourself going down the wrong path. There is a path that's just right for you. Keep going and don't give up, and you will get there.

World-renowned Personal Development Expert Jim Lutes used to say, "If it's meant to be, it's up to me." With that thought in mind, here are just a few people who followed their hearts and their intuition, and made their dreams come true.

MALALA YOUSAFZAI

Malala is a Pakistani female education activist who, at the age of 17, was awarded the 2014 Nobel Peace Prize. She was born on July 12, 1997, in Mingora, Pakistan. Her father was a teacher and ran a girls' school in their village. In January 2008, everything changed when the Taliban took over and banned education for all women. She had to say goodbye to all of her friends and her education. She was only eleven years old. At the young age of fifteen, she took a bold step and spoke out against the unrest in her country, and mostly the right for girls to have an education. In October, 2012, a gunman boarded a bus, found her, and shot her in the head. She woke up ten days later in England with doctors and nurses praising her bravery, excitedly telling her about the support she was gaining worldwide. Malala often says she had a choice to make when she woke up, to either hide in secrecy and safety for the rest of her life, or use this as her platform to fight for equality. She tells all who will listen that her father was her inspiration. Together they created the Malala Fund, an international, non-profit organization that advocates for girls' education all over the world. Malala is one of only two Pakistanis to have ever received the Nobel Prize.

ELON MUSK

Elon is a complex human with a creative brain. He was born in South Africa in the early 1970s to a father who was an engineer and a mother who was a nutritionist. Musk has been quoted as saying that his parents led a busy life so he was raised by books. Isaac Asimov's books caught his attention at a young age and he was hooked on all things space related. He says he can't ever recall a time he didn't have a thirst for learning. He funded all of his own education through odd jobs and loans. He graduated from the University of Pennsylvania with a Bachelor of Science Degree in economics and a Bachelor of Arts degree in physics. Musk has always been willing to work for what he has. His first start-up company, Zip2 took a while to get off the ground and Elon was strapped financially. He slept on the couch in his office and showered at the local gym. This never swayed him from his goal. He was determined to make his dreams a reality. He sold that company earning 22 million dollars at age 27. His first thought was, *how can I invest this money into my next venture?* He soon become the co-founder of PayPal, then moved on to Tesla, and is currently SpaceX Chief Engineer and owner of Twitter. Elon Musk is driven by his passion for technology and for excellence in all things.

OPRAH WINFREY

We all know this beautiful soul as the Queen of talk shows, but how did she get her start and what inspires her? Oprah Winfrey was born on January 29, 1954, in Mississippi to a single teen mom. Her father, Vernon Winfrey, left soon after she was born. At that time, her mom was only 18 years old and had no job. She couldn't take care of her baby, so she left Oprah to live with her maternal grandmother. This is where she would stay for the next six years. She lived the poorest of lifestyles, struggled for food, and had no heat at times.

Oprah's grandmother saw a spark in her very early. She taught her to read when she was only three. At around this same age, Oprah was able to recite Bible passages. She can also remember lining up her dolls and interviewing them. Her grandmother noticed this as well and always encouraged her. Oprah credits her grandmother with pushing her and helping her feel so comfortable speaking publicly. After being bounced around from home to home, she finally settled in with her father and stepmother. They encouraged her reading and speaking skills. She was being asked regularly to speak in church and was even paid $500 at one engagement. She claims that was her turning point. She knew she could be paid to do what she loved. Furthermore, she poured all her love and passion into fine-tuning that skill. The rest is history.

MACK RUTHERFORD

European teen and private pilot Mack Rutherford recently broke the world record for being the youngest pilot to fly solo around the world. He is seventeen years old. He beat the previous record set last year by 18-year-old Travis Ludlow from Britain. Mack has been flying most of his life with his dad, who is also a pilot. He earned his private pilot's certificate when he was only fifteen years old, making him the world's youngest pilot. He has been quoted as saying, "I hope my achievement inspires young people to pursue their dreams" (Toshkov, 2022).

When he stepped out of the aircraft after his around-the-world mission, he said, "Just follow your dreams, no matter how old you are—work hard and move forward to achieve your goals (Toshkov, 2022).

TONI MORRISON

Toni Morrison was a brilliant African American woman who is considered to have been one of the finest authors of her time. Her works were published as fiction, but her stories were based on true accounts of life experiences that other black authors didn't dare write about. In the 2019 documentary about the late author, titled *Toni Morrison, The Pieces I am*, she talks about race and American history in a way no one else I have ever read talks about it.

Morrison faced racism throughout her life and fought hard for her education. She graduated from Howard University and then went on to Cornell for her graduate degree. Morrison later returned to Howard University, where she taught for eight years. After taking a job as an editor at Random House, she began secretly writing her own book and eventually began writing for Alfred A. Knopf, where her career as a novelist really took off. Even though Toni Morrison is considered one of the greatest novelists of her time, she rarely received the acclaim she deserved. However, after she published *Beloved* in 1987, her work could not be ignored.

Beloved spent 25 weeks on the bestseller list and was made into a movie the following year with the help of Oprah Winfrey, who produced and starred in the film. Ms. Morrison was awarded the Pulitzer Prize in Fiction for *Beloved*, even though it was the true story of an African American slave who chose to kill her child rather than allow her to be raised in slavery. When Morrison received the Nobel

Prize for Literature in 1993, she found out about it from a friend who heard about it on the radio.

Morrison attributes her childhood as being an inspiration for her. The struggles both she and her family endured with segregation and racism are depicted in her novels. At the age of two, her family home was burned to the ground by the owner, despite his knowing they were all inside.

So many people of every race, creed, and color, in every walk of life, from every corner of the world, do amazing things every day because they keep on believing, and they don't give up. Why not you?

ENES KANTER FREEDOM

Enes Kanter Freedom is a Swiss-born basketball player who fled Turkey where he was raised, and became an American citizen. He was labeled a terrorist by the Turkish State for speaking out against the Turkish Government's policies. The 11-year NBA veteran played center for the Boston Celtics before being traded to the Houston Rockets.

You might have heard of him from all the press he received about writing messages on his basketball shoes, including "Free Tibet" and "Free Uyghurs" while openly criticizing China for their inhumane practices and civil rights violations. In an interview in December 2022, Enes talked about how he got involved in advocating for human rights for people in China.

Until recently, he was best known for his basketball prowess. Now, however, he is better known as a human rights activist who forfeited a lucrative career with the NBA for speaking out against inhumane practices and civil rights violations in China. Like many NBA players who wrote messages on their basketball shoes, Enes did too. But his messages were bolder than most and immediately caught the attention of the NBA who quickly asked him to avoid messages that criticized the Chinese Regime. NBA China is a $5 billion business with NBA owners' investments there around $10 billion, according to ESPN's website. Since China plays a big role in the NBA, the owners don't want to offend them.

Enes refused to comply and has not been allowed to play, even though he is still a member of the NBA. As a result of his public statements and his refusal to remove the messages from his basketball shoes, he has sacrificed a great deal. Although he refused to retire from professional basketball, he will likely never play again. When asked about his commitment to supporting human rights, in view of what his advocacy has cost him, he stated that anyone can stand up for something if it doesn't cost them anything.

Share the five dynamic principles that can transform a teen's life unequivocally

"Sharing knowledge is the most fundamental act of friendship. Because it is a way you can give something without loosing something."

— Richard Stallman

Earlier in this book, I mentioned that the teen years can be as beautiful as they are challenging.

Teens these days can feel like they are constantly having to put out fires in a myriad of areas—including their academic, social, and family lives.

Thankfully, there is a wide range of skills that can completely transform the way you view yourself and your role in the world. One of these is communication—the ability to not only express yourself assertively, but also listen to others with an open heart and mind. When you are fully present for others, it is difficult not to treasure being by your side.

Panic, anxiety, peer pressure—all the things that make you feel like you don't belong—have no power over your life when you know how to manage your emotions, set goals, and plan ahead.

Connecting with a greater energy, strengthening your faith, and granting unconditional love to others enables you to feel like part of something beautiful and powerful.

In the same way that friends provide an invaluable source of support in times of need, you can alleviate others' pain by sharing the valuable life skills contained in this book.

By leaving a review of this book on Amazon, you'll help other teens and parents stay true to their values and principles, while giving their best selves to others.

Simply by telling them how this book helped you and what they can expect to find inside, you'll help them master the strategies they need to be more communicative, confident, and giving.

https://www.amazon.com/review/create-review/?channel=glance-detail&asin=0966204956&ie=UTF8

CHAPTER 4:
HOW TO PLAN FOR A HAPPY
AND SUCCESSFUL LIFE

If you plan on being anything less than you are capable of being,
you will probably be unhappy all the days of your life.
– Abraham Maslow

ADOLESCENTS/TEENS

I know it can be difficult feeling like you are just floating in limbo while some of your friends already know what they want to do with their lives. Sometimes, if they think you are moving too slowly, parents will try to talk you into following a career path they followed or wanted to follow as a teen but didn't get the chance to. But, even though their intentions are well-meant, this is your life. If you want to do what you love and love what you do, you have to sit up and pay attention. You have to learn how to take responsibility for your own actions and make some of your own decisions.

There is no need to get all stressed out and panicky about it. It takes some people longer to find their special path than it does others. You can carry a small notebook, or use your phone, and write down ideas when they pop into your mind. If you don't write them down, you'll forget them. I recommend one of those little spiral-bound notebooks. You don't need anyone else to see your dreams and goals right now. Keep your creative energy and ideas to yourself, if you want to make them happen. There are talkers and doers. Save your energy for the doing. Keep paying attention and writing down those ideas that make you stop and think. It will be worth it, I promise.

Having a blueprint to follow will reduce the stress and anxiety that comes with not knowing what's going to happen next. You make the plan, follow the steps, set priorities and boundaries. It is important to care about others, but don't give what you don't have. Be very conscious of how you spend your time and energy. Work the plan until it gets you where you want to go. When you do the things that support your mission and life goals, you will be able to handle whatever comes along because you will be fulfilling your purpose in life. Living a life that makes you happy is the best success anyone can hope for.

Everyone needs a life plan that is designed especially for them. One of the most important things for a teen to have is an open mind. A growth mindset is necessary for success. Make room for new ideas and notice what works and what doesn't. Many things will change - goals, priorities, mission, friends, and passions - on your path to success. Your definition of success might change, too, as you get older and your life circumstances change. Having a growth mindset when you're young will equip you with the success tools you'll need throughout your life. There are many ways to do things and many ways to achieve a goal. Your job is to decide which way is best for you and then do it.

There are all kinds of goals. There are short-term goals, long-term goals, and lifetime goals. There are different schools of thought on the timeline for accomplishing different goals, but this is my version. Short-term goals are usually 1-3 months, but they can take up to 6 months. I skip the mid-term category because it reminds me of micro-managing, and that can cause unnecessary anxiety. Long-term goals can take anywhere from 3-5 years. Lifetime goals are just that, things you want to do for your entire life.

As you read through this list of potential goals, write next to each goal if you think it is long-term (LT), short-term (ST), or lifetime (L). Use the above timeline to help you decide which is which. Also, some goals may fit into two or even all three categories.

I've listed a few potential goals to get you started. There are many more, so if you don't see yours on the list, write them in the blank spaces.

- play varsity football
- be a cheerleader
- open your own auto repair business
- study music at Julliard

- ask someone out on a date
- get your homework completed on time
- make the honor roll
- get your own car
- move into your own apartment
- learn how to make your own clothes
- get a pet
- get a job doing something you really like
- make a difference in the world
- volunteer at a place where you can meet people with similar interests
- play a musical instrument
- fly an airplane
- make movies
- become a paramedic, nurse, doctor, plumber, or electrician
- teach school
- run for office
- start a YouTube channel
- start your online business
- travel the world
- _____
- _____
- _____
- _____

I'm sure you can think of more. I'm also sure you can achieve at least five of the goals you choose, once you decide what is important to you and create a plan that supports each goal. You don't need to do everything at once. Pick the most important goal to you right now and work on that one. Keep going, one by one, step by step, and before you know it, you will be there.

Different goals have different timelines, as we discussed earlier, so in some cases it is possible to work on more than one goal at one time. You can usually work on a short-term goal at the same time as a long-term goal, especially when the short-term goal is one of the steps leading to a long-term goal. You are always focusing on the short-term goals because those are the ones you need to do now, and the baby steps are the ones that allow you to go the distance. This is where priorities and goals meet. We'll talk more about priorities in Chapter 5.

Each time you achieve a short-term goal, such as playing varsity football, you are working toward your long-term goal of playing college football. You can double your accomplishments with one effort. If you have another long-term goal of playing for the NFL, then both of the previous goals will be part of that plan. If you are like Tom Brady, it might even become a lifetime goal. The same thing would apply if you want to study music at Julliard and eventually play for a symphony or choreograph Broadway musicals. You would start with a short-term goal like playing a musical instrument or studying dance.

Make up your mind to do one thing every day that will bring you closer to your goal. Write it down in a full sentence. "This is what I did today to work toward my goal of _____" and fill in the blank. This simple self-discipline will remind you of your commitment and your accomplishments.

It's kind of funny, after trying custom apps and programs, fancy notebooks, and other impressive planning tools, I finally ended up with a simple college-ruled, spiral-bound notebook that I keep on my desk and use daily. I met a friend of mine for lunch one day to exchange notes on a project we were discussing. I was surprised to see this business executive who has a briefcase that probably cost more than my computer, open it and take out a spiral-bound notebook just like mine. He said he had used it for twenty years and had never found a system that worked better. Find whatever works for you and use it.

You probably already know this, but I'm going to say it anyway. Any time you try something new, there's a chance that it won't work the first time. Maybe you won't even like the goal after you try it. No worries. It's okay and even healthy to change your mind when the signs indicate that you are going in the wrong direction. If it doesn't feel right, cross it off your list and move on to the next goal. Sometimes knowing what you *don't* want to do helps you figure out what you *do* want to do.

If you get stuck, resist the urge to let your parents jump in and fix "the problem", even though they might try to do that. It may not be a problem to you, just a temporary setback that you are perfectly capable of working through yourself. Let your parents know if you truly need their help by asking them. However, if it *is* something you are capable of doing yourself, then do it yourself. If your parents insist, simply look them in the eye, tell them "no", smile, and thank them for offering to help. It's a great way to end the conversation and avoid a negative outcome. Then put your mind, body, intuition, and talents to good use and get it done.

How to Choose and Set Goals

Here are a few important things to consider when you are setting your goals. First of all, even though you will accomplish many things in your life, the things that are most important to you will never be urgent. When I say urgent, I mean things like getting your pet to the vet after it has been hit by a car, or studying hard so you can get a good grade on your test tomorrow or else you will lose a scholarship opportunity. Those are important things that are urgent. You have to do them NOW.

But there are other things that are important to you in your life that are *not* urgent. If you want them to happen, you have to *make* them urgent. These are the goals that, when you achieve them, will make your dreams come true. You might have noticed them on the list of potential goals, maybe you have a poster or a list that you keep in your bedroom to inspire you as you work to make them part of your life plan. You have to create an urgency around them and make them so important that you can't not put in the work.

Write Down Your Goals

There are certain things to consider when you are writing down your goals. You might want to brainstorm with someone or just yourself. Write down everything you can think of that you would love to do, whether it seems within your reach or not. You don't have to wait until you're grown up to dream big. There are many goals you can achieve as a young person striving for something you love. Write them all down. Don't hold back.

Now, read all of those goals you wrote down out loud, and choose the ones that you like the best and want to work on first. Put a check mark by them. Remember, choose four or five. You can work on the rest later. Start with what is most important to you or what might be easiest for you to achieve. Your confidence will build with each goal you achieve.

Goal-setting consists of a few steps that will make your plan work better for you. Goals should be:

Clearly stated. That list of all kinds of goals, even the crazy ones, can be narrowed down to four or five things. You can always add others after you achieve the first ones.

Achievable. There has to be some level of achievement you are anticipating so you can work on ways to get there. Your "dream" goals may seem unrealistic to some but I'm sure you can think of many things that "couldn't be done" that are being done every day. Don't ever be afraid to dream big.

Measurable and Trackable. You have to be able to measure your progress so you can track your goal along its timeline and determine when you have achieved it.

Have a timeline. How long will it take you to achieve the goal? Is it a short-term goal that you can achieve in three months, or a long-term goal that might need many steps before you actually achieve it? A short-term goal might be to make the Honor Roll, take driving lessons, or get a part-time job. Some examples of long-term goals might be to become a professional dancer or athlete, get a master's degree or doctorate you can use to become a teacher, scientist, engineer, or psychologist. It could also be a law degree, or a nursing or medical degree, or becoming an entrepreneur so you will one day own your own business.

Let your mission, your purpose, and your reason for being guide you. Find out everything you can about your prospective career goals before you talk to your parents. Do your homework. They might object to your choices for various reasons, but if you show them that you have researched the options thoroughly, they will probably listen, even if they don't agree. Most parents want what's best for their children, which doesn't always match what you think is best for you. Be respectful and listen.

Your parents want you to make a good living so you can give your children all the things your parents could not give you. What can I say? It's a parent thing. It can be hard for parents to listen to your dreams and desires unless they involve making a lot of money because most people believe that if you have a lot of money, you will be happy. Underneath it all, parents really do want their children to be happy. Being happy may not mean the same thing to you as it does to your parents, so work on your plan and always have a backup. And no matter what happens, don't give up. Try not to let your dream get lost in whatever career you choose. You can always do it on the side, but don't forget about it.

You can change your plan any time you want. You will be adding to it and redefining it often, but if you follow it, it will work. Don't be afraid to change your mind. Don't worry about how many times it doesn't work until it finally does. Your life is a work in progress, so your life plan must be flexible enough to keep up, yet focused enough to stay on track. If you follow your life plan and lead with your heart, you will succeed. And you will be happy.

PARENTS
Please read the quote under the photo above. Abraham Maslow is best known for Maslow's Hierarchy of Needs. It's a wonderful

quote. How often do we give up on our adolescents and teens when they stubbornly resist doing things our way? I don't expect people to be more than they are, but I won't encourage them to be less, and that includes teenagers. Our adolescents and teens deserve our support, and they need it to thrive.

There are many ways to do things, and what works well for us may not work at all for them. When I see ideas from a young mind produce outcomes I would have never even thought of, it makes me realize how easy it is to become narrowminded. As parents, we must be willing to look at ideas other than our own and remember that lifelong learning is to be admired and appreciated. We can learn much from our adolescents and teens and still be the person in charge. Being in charge doesn't mean you have to control everything. It means that we're the ones who are responsible for the young people entrusted to our care. We are parents and we are not perfect. And that's okay.

CHAPTER 5:
PRIORITIZING—
HOW TO DECIDE WHAT TO DO FIRST

When you know what is important to you,
making a decision is quite easy.
−Anthony Robbins

ADOLESCENTS/TEENS

When you look at your life plan, you'll be able to see where you are heading. You may change your route along the way, but the things that are truly important to you will most likely remain truly important. Make sure you spend time on those goals and don't allow yourself to get sidetracked by urgent but unimportant texts, calls, and unplanned entertainment. It's easy for someone else's wishes to take you away from your very important goals.

One of the biggest challenges for teens is to be able to say "No" to their friends. You don't want to be rude but it might be a good idea to ask yourself, "Will doing this right now make my life better"? This simple question brings you back into the moment and gives you a chance to let your intuition kick in before you answer. "Let me think about it" is a good way to check with your intuition before you make your choice.

Your answer might be "yes". Keep an open mind and give yourself a chance to respond instead of reacting without thinking and going along with the crowd, convincing yourself you will get the important things done later. You could go through your entire lifetime and never get to do the things you truly love, if you wait until they become urgent.

You probably know people like that, maybe even your parents. Parents and most other people in your life will tell you sacrifices are part of life if you want to get the things you want. Parents want a good life for their children, but when you're a teen, you are not thinking about them. You are thinking about you. The teenage years are overwhelming.

How can you possibly share your parents' perspective? You haven't lived long enough to know what they learned, so you have to go with what you have learned so far. Parents sometimes see their teens as know-it-alls but you can only pour so much knowledge into a person. When there is no more room for more learning, you have to wait until your life experiences catch up and give you the wisdom to match what you have learned. The wisdom will spill out into life and you can start filling up the knowledge jar again.

Everyone is a know-it-all at some stage of life. As we acquire humility, we discover that the more we learn, the less we know.

That is when life's adventure requires you to do the things that you can't put off until later, the really important things that will make your life wonderful.

Sacrificing does not include sacrificing yourself because of guilt, or thinking maybe you don't deserve the life you want. You do deserve it. So, go for it.

Sometimes it is hard to know where to start and what to do first. Setting priorities can be an overwhelming task. You can't do everything at once so you have to pick and choose what is most important in your life, and decide the order in which you will proceed.

TEENS/PARENTS

There are also the highest priorities of all to consider. These are the foundation for your life and how you choose to live it. These priorities usually do not change during your lifetime. They become a part of you as you grow and develop, and they influence all your other priorities.

The top priorities for most people are Family, School, Work, and God, not necessarily in that order. Let's look at each of them.

Family

What does it mean when you say that family comes first? What actions support this?

Do you sit down together for a meal with no cell phones, and talk to each other while sharing a meal?

Parents, do you make sure you are present for your adolescents' and teens' school plays, football games, recitals, awards ceremonies, and school conferences?

Do you have a reasonable set of house rules that include sharing chores, outlining curfews, and other expectations so that everyone knows what is expected? (Parents and teens should share this activity so it is fair and respectful to everyone involved.)

Teens, do you make sure your parents know where you are and how to contact you in an emergency? I know you usually have your cell phone, but what if you didn't?

School

For the adolescent and teen, school is a top priority. So what actions support this?

Do you study and complete your homework on time?

Do you set an alarm so you can wake up on time and get to school on time?

Do you contribute in class and participate in class projects?

Do you get to practice on time for music, sports, school clubs, and other activities that occur outside of school hours?

Do you let your parents know about meetings you are planning to attend and what time these activities take place?

Work
If you have a part-time job, do you make sure you are clean and dressed neatly for it?

Do you arrive on time, do your job well and act in a trustworthy manner?

Are you polite to customers and helpful when possible?

Are you someone your boss can depend on?

Do you enjoy your job? This is important because if you like what you do, you will probably do a better job.

God
For many people, their spiritual life is their first priority. Their belief and trust in God as the Creator of the Universe, the Source of all things, is what brings harmony, peace, and meaning to their lives. However, not everyone goes to church or believes in a Creator, or a Supreme Being by any name. I use the name "God" because it is the name I prefer to call the Creator of All Things. I have heard there are thousands of names for God, but I only know a few.

If you don't go to church, there is nothing wrong with that. However, it is important to understand that faith is a powerful tool, and you deserve to know about it if you don't already. Your connection to your inner self allows your intuition to open many doors your mind cannot. This connection is discussed more in Chapter Six.

Changing Priorities

Priorities sometimes need to be shifted from time to time. Most of the time, you will be working on whatever is important at that moment. For instance, school or family might be more important than your job on a particular day. You might have to ask your boss for the night off so you can study for a test, or attend your sibling's dance recital.

If you are feeling anxious and confused about what to do first when goals seem to be competing for your attention, stop for a moment. Set your phone down or better yet, turn it off. Sit down, relax, close your eyes, take three deep breaths, and ask yourself, "What is the most important thing I need to do right now?" Then fall silent. It may take asking yourself two or three times. Use the breaths to clear your head, like in a meditation. Then just sit there for a minute or two. Your answer will come to you. Do that thing and then move on. No need for anxiety. Decision removes anxiety, and if you make a poor decision, you can always make another one.

When deciding which task to do first, I use a principle I learned from a wise and successful real estate entrepreneur. His motto was "Feared Things First." The idea is that if you can pick the thing you dread doing the most and do it first, then everything you do afterward will seem easy. It works for me.

There is something called "shared priorities". At least that's what I call them. Each of you will have your personal priorities and they will be different because, as a family, you have different jobs to do. Shared Priorities are the things that are important to both parents and teens. There are only a few. Ask your Mom or Dad sometime, "What is something that's really important to you?" This is a very personal question, so after you ask it, don't speak, just wait for an answer. They will answer. Whatever they say, you reply, "Okay, thank you." And parents, I offer you the same advice.

ADOLESCENTS/TEENS

Be clear about what is really important to you. When you set your priorities, you also have to set boundaries. For example, it's pretty hard to get any studying done when someone is blowing up your phone with text messages that can wait until later. In order to get anything accomplished, you need to give your full attention to the task at hand. In other words, please get rid of all the distractions so you can focus and get it done.

If your friends can't resist texting you and you cannot resist answering each one, turn off your phone. Then, you can tell them you won't be available between the hours of so-and-so and such-and-such.

Here in this techno-modern world, people run around like crazy, doing more and more unnecessary things and letting others decide who they're supposed to be. There is something to be said for un-hurriedness, for appreciating what you have and staying in the moment so you can take advantage of all the possibilities right there in front of you.

Your life has its own pace. Enjoy the ride. What's the point of all that hard work and discipline if you can't enjoy your dream or even recognize it when it's right there in your hand? All that rushing around only leads to anxiety and feelings of not enough, which is not exactly a recipe for success.

Lastly, I'd like to share with you two things that helped me tremendously when I was setting goals and creating a life plan. One was from Steven R. Covey's book, "The 7 Habits of Highly Effective People". It was "Habit 2: Begin with the end in mind." You can find it online or in the library. The second was a quote from Napoleon Hill, whose most famous book is "Think and Grow Rich." "Plan your work and work your plan." I learned more about setting and achieving goals by following those two pieces of advice than anything else I can remember.

Follow your plan at your pace, and prioritize your tasks. Don't be afraid to change your priorities when your plan calls for it or if your goals change. This is one time you need to put your own needs first. It's not selfish. You have to take care of yourself so you will have the extra energy to care for somebody else.

CHAPTER 6:
TAKE TIME TO CONNECT

Sometimes, you find yourself in the middle of nowhere,
and, sometimes, in the middle of nowhere you find yourself.
–Author Unknown

TEENS/PARENTS

This chapter stresses the importance of strengthening your inner connection in order to tap into the vast inner resources that are available to all humans. Teenagers, like adults, need time away from the noise and the clutter of the expectations and demands of others. This includes social media, peer pressure, cell phones, and other time and energy thieves. Quieting the mind through meditation, prayer, or simply being out in Nature, allows us to tap into vast inner resources.

I know this may be going against the norm, but it's okay to pray. Prayer is simply talking to God, who has many names, or angels, or a Saint or the Blessed Mother, or any other spiritual being we might happen to feel a connection with. It is not necessary to go to church to believe or acknowledge that there is something greater than us in the world.

Scientific evidence has proven that meditation is effective in reducing stress and anxiety, reducing negative emotions, increasing imagination and creativity, promoting emotional health, and lengthening attention span. The Mayo Clinic, and many other health organizations, have confirmed this.

Learn to play, have fun, and express joy. Nature, away from cell phones and daily noise, is a wonderful playground. Away from the noise, mind-cluttering social media and other distractions, activities like camping, hiking, kayaking, biking, fishing, lying on the ground and looking up at the sky, or just walking in the woods or a field, encourage connection at the deepest level. Research has found that Nature is extremely beneficial to teen health.

Connection is a concept that is often misunderstood. Connection has to do with a source of energy that flows through everyone and everything. You can connect with this energy and tap into your intuition to find answers to most of the questions in your life. It supports and energizes you.

This kind of energy doesn't come from a sports drink, or a drug, or any other outside influence. It comes from inside you, from your heart. It is mighty powerful, and everyone has access to it. Some teenagers may not be aware of this since it is not technological or even logical. It has nothing to do with your mind or your brain. It is that part of you which is more than enough. It is who you are. And how does this energy work?

Well, you know how when you plug in Christmas lights, and they light up when the plug connects to the outlet in the wall? Humans are connected like that, too. We don't need a chip installed in our body to connect with ourselves or each other. We are already connected to an invisible energy, what some people call the Source or God. This connection, this power, comes from within us, not from an outside source. No one can see it or explain it, but you can feel it. We can tap into it any time we want. We are connected to everyone and everything on the planet. That includes plants, animals, trees, grass, the oceans and rivers and, of course, other human beings. We all have that invisible energy, that essence of life, flowing through us, just like the energy that flows through those light bulbs when they are plugged in. We are just plugging into our heart energy, an inside source of energy, like the strand of lights plugs into an electrical outlet, an outside source of energy.

In the case of a strand of Christmas lights, one or two lights can go out and the rest stay lit. There is a slight disconnect but the other lights help keep the rest of the strand lit. By the way, did you ever notice how often people focus on that one dark light rather than all the other beautiful ones that are still lit? Sometimes we focus so hard on the things that used to be that we forget all about the bright things that are here right now. If we do that long enough, we can get lost in the darkness and lose our way.

When we disconnect from the energy source and unplug, the light goes out, and darkness sets in. Some people don't like winter because they need sunlight to keep them in a light space. As a result, they can feel very down when it is gloomy outside. There is a term for this. It's called Seasonal Affective Disorder (SAD). That's how a person feels when they are disconnected from the sunlight for periods of time. The same thing can happen with your heart light.

Think about the light as love and the darkness as fear. Our minds react to these feelings. You don't worry about things when you are tuned in and connected. Your intuition guides you to the light again. We talked about intuition earlier in Chapter 3.

Sometimes something big happens in your life, and the light can be reduced to a tiny spark. You may feel like the light has gone out because heartache feels like that. But there is always a spark in there somewhere, and you can reconnect with it.

I have listed below a few of the things that can try to darken your day and make you feel alone and forgotten. Don't let them steal your joy. It's okay to feel sad when bad things happen. Sometimes it hurts so bad that you feel like you can't go on, but this is a time when connecting to yourself and those who love you is more important than ever.

- Friends and family who don't support you or believe in you
- Stressful changes at home, like moving, a death, or divorce
- Trauma or abuse that we sometimes hide from others
- Being around negative people who make you uncomfortable about feeling happy
- Unhealthy practices like overeating or using alcohol or drugs

Any of these things can threaten to disconnect you from the safe, comfortable, joyful connection we were all born with. This connection is a necessary part of your growth and development into a wholesome, happy, human being. The threat alone is pressure enough to push teenagers into a depression, which leads to more loneliness and isolation. It is a cycle that is very difficult to break. Don't wait too long to reach out to someone for help when you need it.

FAITH
TEENS/PARENTS
Faith is the very short name for a very big belief system. Faith is believing in something you cannot see or explain. It is complete trust and confidence in someone. In most cases, this is God, but really, it's also your parents, friends, pets, and yourself. The one I call God is the Creator of all things. To one of my friends, it is the Great Spirit; to another, it is Allah; to yet another it is simply The Source. God has many names and many faithful servants. Faith is a feeling you feel in your heart, not in your mind.

Faith was a given when I was growing up. Most everyone I know went to church. It was a great source of strength and community. Prayer was part of our lives. When things got chaotic, we had people who knew about God. We read the Bible or other spiritual works and did our best to be kind, good people. Faith gives one a sense of peace and stability. The family unit was very important, and we found comfort in knowing that another person felt that spiritual bond, just as we did. It joined us as a community of people who supported each other, didn't give up on each other, and were not afraid to love each other.

Our world has changed, and it continues to change at an alarmingly rapid pace. We spend more time alone than ever before, and in those quiet moments, if we feel scared, anxious, or depressed, who do we reach for? The people we leaned on for love and support when I was young are not in the picture for most young people today. Many young people do not know God and feel they have only themselves to depend on.

Our mental health is constantly disrupted by gadgets, negative news, and unsafe surroundings. A debilitating doctrine of fear appears to be consuming the planet. We cannot keep ignoring it. We took this odd turn away from faith, and now many criticize people who hold onto theirs. Many parents do not go to church anymore, and I'm not saying that they should. But there is more to life than what is programmed into your cell phone. And faith is a pretty good thing to have when the going gets rough.

When I was young, I went to Catholic Mass every Sunday with my family. Afterward, we went back home and had ham and eggs, and biscuits with jelly, all homemade, and then went about our day. It was part of our life, and I loved it. I spent a lot of time at our church when I was growing up. It makes me sad to think that today's teens and their entire generation are missing out on faith. They are lost and struggling—we know this. Having a sense of faith, warmth, compassion, and love, would go a long way. Even though I no longer attend a regular religious service, I take God with me wherever I go.

"The Exchange Zone" is a phrase coined by Christian author and minister Christine Caine, from Australia, who also wrote "Unstoppable". Although my beliefs are not exactly like hers, I do believe in God and I have come to know that miracles are all around us. I think young people might find hope in some of her work, even if they do not follow a Christian teaching. "The Exchange Zone" is a faith-based book and teaching about how we must pass the baton of faith on to the next person or generation so they can know God and all the miracles that can happen in our lives. There is a darkness surrounding our youth today and political correctness makes some authors shy away from this topic, but I believe it is a missing component in the lives of too many young people, so I want to share it.

I do not pretend that I know better than others in some areas of life. We can only speak from our own perspective which comes from the wisdom we have gained from our own life adventures. But God is something I know about, so I will share my thoughts with you. Then, you can do with them what you want.

As you read through this book, or any other, for that matter, or listen to the audiobook, you will read and hear things that make sense to you and that you will find helpful. You will also read and hear things that you disagree with. Don't let the things that don't resonate with you prevent you from learning about the things you find helpful. There is no right way or wrong way to learn. Until you can put what you've learned into action, it is wise to go with what you feel comfortable with at any given time. Don't get hung up on the things that you don't like. Let them go and focus on the things that make sense to you in your life. Use what you can, and don't worry about the rest, okay?

NATURE REDUCES ANXIETY AND COUNTERACTS SCREEN TIME

Did you know that the average American teenager spends nine hours in front of a screen every day? And 50% of teens, when asked, say they feel addicted to their devices (Monroe, 2018).

So how do you counteract the effects of all that screen time? Nature can help. By now, you probably know how much I love Nature. When we take the time to unplug from technology and tune in to our surroundings in a natural setting, our mood improves and we develop a sense of calm. Constant chaos doesn't help anyone. It never has and it never will. Being in nature restores mental energy that has been zapped away by technology.

Nature is full of all kinds of healthy entertainment. There's kayaking, hiking, bike riding, skating, skateboarding, tubing, fishing, swimming, water-skiing, snowboarding in the winter, wind-surfing, playing Frisbee, walking along the lake or the beach, or just throwing a ball around or resting peacefully in the sun or shade.

Why not spend some time with your friends outdoors? Nature is beautiful and full of life. When you connect with Nature, you're connecting with life. Breathe in that fresh air and feel the fullness of life. You're part of that. There is a contentment you can only find in Nature because you naturally become part of the positive energy. Letting go of negative energy by embracing Mother Nature and all her gifts will change your entire perspective.

I suspect you will have to take your phone with you, so take lots of great pictures to post for your friends. Maybe they will join you the next time.

CHAPTER 7:
FIVE DYNAMIC LIFE PRINCIPLES THAT CAN CHANGE YOUR LIFE FOREVER

ADOLESCENTS/TEENS

Make no mistake, your life is going to change all by itself. We are all energy, and energy is always in motion. In this chapter, we are going to discuss five things you can do every day to help you flow with the changes as they happen. You can use these five dynamic life principles to help you cope with the stress and anxiety that often accompany change. Please understand that this is a life-long learning process which will benefit you in many ways, not only now in your younger years, but throughout your entire life. So be patient and persistent.

Now, let's take a close look at these five dynamic life principles that you can use to create a happy and successful life for yourself.

DYNAMIC LIFE PRINCIPLE #1: GRANT UNCONDITIONAL LOVE TO EVERYONE
PARENTS AND TEENS

Unconditional love is the greatest gift we can give ourselves and others. It is Divine Love, the kind that accepts you as you are, the kind of love that doesn't judge you. It is like the tender love of a child who trusts you completely and thinks you're perfect just the way you are.

There are many who believe that unconditional love is the answer to all questions and the solution to all problems. I am one of those people. Unconditional love is the secret for living a happy and successful life. There is a common divinity in all people. Unconditional love is more powerful than any other force in the Universe. It is the one life skill we simply cannot thrive without. It makes everything possible.

I mentioned Lester Levenson, author and creator of The Sedona Method, further developed by his successor, Hale Dwoskin, in another chapter. His observation about people and love is worth sharing. He said that all happiness equates to one's capacity to love, while all misery equates to one's need to be loved. Think about that for a moment. "All misery equates to one's need to be loved." How great is your capacity to love? How do you feel at those times when you need love and no one seems to want to love you? Everyone needs to be loved, not just by others but by themselves, too.

Self-love includes self-acceptance. Learning to love and accept yourself is no easy task. You are too young to remember this, but in

1986, a beautiful young woman named Whitney Houston released a song titled, *The Greatest Love of All*. I can't think of too many songs that are more powerful and empowering than that one. I still love to hear it after all these years. I know it inspired and even saved a lot of teens back then. It is as relevant today as it was then. Listen to it some time when you get a chance, and you'll know what I mean.

Loving yourself means loving the person you are and the person you are becoming. Don't be too hard on yourself. You might tell yourself that if you were better, prettier, smarter, slimmer, or had two parents, then you would fit in and be happy. But truth be told, unless you can accept yourself with all your delightful imperfections, you will not be able to accept others as they are either. Unconditional love comes from the inside out. Without unconditional love and self-acceptance, no matter how many things you achieve in your lifetime, you will always feel like something is missing.

You don't have to do anything spectacular to be worthy of love. It takes humility to admit that you are perfect just the way you are. Yep, and you were created that way for a reason. You're no mistake. You're you, the only "YOU" in the whole Universe. No one can do "YOU" better than you. It is simply not possible.

We are constantly comparing ourselves to others' ideas of what perfection is. Unconditional love is you showing up as yourself. You don't need to change yourself so you can fit in. You are unique and wonderful. You will have more confidence, and life will be more fun, and a gazillion other things you can't even imagine right now, when you show up as yourself. The famous fashion designer, Coco Chanel, once said that beauty begins the moment you decide to be yourself.

We are all different human beings. You are beautiful inside and out, and I know you hate to hear that because most of us were taught conditional love. That's the kind of love that says, "It's okay. I love you anyway." Who wants to be loved "anyway"? Instead of trying to identify all of your shortcomings, be happy and grateful for all that you are. When someone criticizes you, including authority figures, look them straight in the eye, give them a big smile—a fake one is okay in this case—and say "Thank you". Then walk away with your head held high.

The last thing I want to say about unconditional love is that granting it to someone doesn't mean you will be close personal friends for life or that you want to go out with the person. It is a quiet acceptance of others even if their lives are different from yours. When you do something nice for someone for no good reason, you are granting them unconditional love. Not everyone is ready to accept unconditional love and you must never put yourself in a dangerous situation because you are trying to be kind. It's okay to make that choice when you are an adult, but not while you are still learning how life works. Love yourself, and everything else will fall into place.

DYNAMIC LIFE PRINCIPLE #2: PRACTICE SELF-DISCIPLINE

Self-discipline is how you train yourself to do what is required to get you to where you want to be. Discipline isn't meant to be a negative term although it is often used in that context. Instead, it's doing the right things consistently and on purpose, so you can stay on track while accomplishing things that matter to you. Self-discipline helps you reach your goals by avoiding the temptation of distracting yourself with useless information and activities that keep you from reaching those goals.

Self-discipline means you keep the promises you make to yourself. There isn't someone standing over you with a stick threatening you and telling you what a loser you will be if you don't do this or that. It's your plan, so it's up to you. Your friends can support you without trying to convince you that it can't hurt to abandon your plan just this once. After all, you work so hard. That's right, you do. And that's precisely why you need to discipline yourself to stay on track. There will be stopping points when you can visit with your friends without breaking your stride. Remember your priorities.

The word "discipline" comes from the word "disciple," which comes from the Latin word "discipulus" which means "student". When you practice self-discipline, you are being the student and the teacher all at once. You don't need to wait to be told what to do and when and how to do it. You have already thought about all of that and gotten a lot of information about it when you were mapping out your goals. You can make those decisions on your own. You make that promise to yourself, and you keep it. If you fall off the wagon once in a while, so what? Just start up again. All is not lost. You don't need to abandon your goal or dream. Just pick up where you left off and carry on.

Self-discipline helps you stay true to yourself and your purpose or mission in life. You can practice it in all areas of your life. It will eventually become a habit and something you will actually want to do. You will be amazed by all the things you will accomplish.

DYNAMIC LIFE PRINCIPLE #3: STAY TRUE TO YOURSELF AND YOUR MISSION

How do you stay true to yourself when you don't even know what that means? And many of you don't. You are still getting to know yourself and you may not have enough information to go on.

Staying true to yourself means doing what your heart tells you is the right thing to do. It doesn't matter what you tell yourself, who tries to convince you, or the mental gymnastics you go through to justify doing something else. Your intuition is whispering to you, but it will sound like it is shouting so loud that you can't hear anything else. You will know the right thing to do. You just have to find the courage to do it.

We haven't talked about integrity, but you have probably heard the word before. When you have integrity, you are committed to doing the right thing. It's part of who you are, part of your character. This is a choice you can make, and different people choose differently. Remember when I talked about keeping your promises to yourself? Well, this is part of that. Even when it's hard, even when the people you counted on don't show up for you, and even if you are scared to stand alone when you know deep inside that this is the right thing to do, you do it.

When you live your life that way, you become a person people trust to tell them the truth, to show up when you say you will, and to inspire them to be better people. You become a true leader, someone who keeps their word, doesn't make excuses or blame others, shows how to help make the world a better place, and *makes* the world a better place just by being in it.

Your goals and life plan will help you figure out what you want to do with your life. After you achieve a few of your goals and then go on to others, there will be one or two things that stand out above the rest. When you work on those goals or even think of them, you will feel the passion build in your heart, and suddenly, in one moment, you will know exactly what you want to do with your life. You will even feel that it is what you are meant to do. Whatever it may be, it will show up in its own good time. Things don't always happen on our timetable, but they always happen at the right time. Be patient and put one foot in front of the other, one step at a time, and you will be ready when the time comes.

Your purpose can reveal itself before or after you find your mission. You might have more than one mission. It might be saving your neighborhood, advocating for better housing, farmer's rights, or the rights of teens. Whatever it turns out to be, it will require action. That means work and the willingness to learn and make a few sacrifices to help achieve the goals of your mission. Once you decide to take it on, your sense of commitment to your mission can be so compelling that you will be hardly able to think of anything else. You will feel a great determination to go after whatever it is you want to go after. Your purpose at that moment will be to fulfill your mission.

There are many people who did this in their lives. Some of them we discussed earlier in Chapter 3. There are others, too, like Mother Teresa, Nelson Mandela, Dolores Huerta, Ryan White who became the face of public education about AIDS when he was 11 years old, Aiden Dwyer who invented a solar tree when he was only 13 years old, and Marley Diaz, a 14-year-old activist and feminist who started a movement to promote diverse representation when she was only 11 years old. There are many others, too, and I encourage you to take the time to check them out. They are the ones who acted on their goals, and made it their mission to share their message with the world because they believed it was the right thing to do. They did not waver. They did what was required and remained true to themselves and their mission in the process. Maybe one day, you will inspire someone like they did. It could happen.

DYNAMIC LIFE PRINCIPLE #4: BE GRATEFUL

We all have something to be grateful for, even you. It might not be something you think about very much but take two or three minutes to look around you and see if you can find something that made your day better today. What is something that happened today that you're glad about?

Sometimes we don't notice things we are glad we have until they are gone. So many things come our way that we just brush off without noticing. Perhaps it is an unexpected smile from someone, the person who helped you pick up your books when you dropped them, someone on the bus that let you get off before them, or the one who reminded you about the test tomorrow when you still had time to go back and get your book so you could take it home to study.

Even the tiniest kindness can change your life when you have an attitude of gratitude. Don't hold back on your gratitude. The more thankful you are for what you already have, the more abundance will come your way. You'll find yourself smiling and enjoying life a lot more, too.

What is an attitude of gratitude? What exactly does this mean? The formal definition of this term is: An attitude of gratitude refers to making a conscious habit of expressing appreciation on a regular basis for both big and small things (Boys Town, 2019). We may be grateful for our family, our friends, our pets, material items, food in our cupboards, our comfortable bed, and our overall sense of well-being.

But is there more to it than that? Yes, there is. Approaching life with an attitude of gratitude will have positive effects on your life now and in the future. It's easy to get down on life, and it's easy to stay there. Be grateful you have a Mom who listens to what you say and doesn't mind letting you talk until you figure things out on your own. Be grateful if you have a friend who likes the same movies you do and enjoys spending time with you even if you are not dating. Be grateful for sunny days and soft breezes that make you close your eyes and take deep breaths and feel peaceful, even if it's only for a moment.

Sometimes, we forget about all the good things we have. They may not seem all that special because we are used to them. But, once in a while, write them down. What was one thing today that made you feel glad? Think about it. Write one thing down each day and you will be amazed by how awesome your life really is when you take a good look at it.

Then, take it one step further. Reach out and help someone else. Give them something to feel grateful about. They may be thinking the same thing you were and you can help them develop that same attitude of gratitude into a habit that will serve you throughout your entire life.

Helping others builds character and gives you a sense of community. Pitch in and contribute to the well-being of someone else. Our human spirit needs to be recharged periodically. Showing love through helping others is a great way to reenergize.

The more love you give, the more you get. It actually feels like you are filling up your soul. It tends to make your life bigger and better. Too many people opt for a small screen life but, with such limited vision, they can only see a small piece of sky. Why not go big so you can see the greater 360-degree vision? It's there. Fire up your imagination. Just look around.

Have you ever volunteered before? It's a great way to exercise your teamwork and leadership skills, and you can make some great friends. There are many ways to volunteer, and plenty of local organizations that can use the help. You'll get a chance to develop skills and uncover talents you didn't even know you had. It can feel awkward in the beginning, but you will gain so much from it that it's worth the temporary discomfort.

If you love pets, see if the animal shelter can use some help. I would recommend a no-kill shelter. Local aviation groups always need volunteers to help at fly-ins and, if you love aircraft, it's fantastically fun. Food banks need help boxing up donations as well. Soup kitchens feed the homeless and are nearly always understaffed. Local churches are also great places to ask because the members are usually well-connected and know of many places in the community that could use a helping hand. If you already belong to a particular church, there are many things you can do to contribute. You can learn a lot working with church groups.

Find your passion and find a way to give back. Your heart will overflow with love, and you just may find a calling while you are at it. Be open to all possibilities, and don't forget to share the things you are experiencing with your parents.

I know working and being useful aren't very popular concepts these days, but if you have talents and skills—and dreams—why not put them to work for you? Hard work never hurt anybody, and it doesn't even feel like work when you're doing something you love. Besides that, it feels wonderful being somebody's champion.

DYNAMIC LIFE PRINCIPLE #5: BE WILLING TO FORGIVE

Forgiveness is about letting go. There is no point in trying to control a situation you have no control over, like someone else's behavior, for instance. Continued practice of this dynamic principle will save you from many heartaches. If you want a full life, forgiveness is the key.

This is not to say that someone who has harmed you deserves your personal attention in the forgiveness process. It does not condone what they did and forgiving them is not saying that it was okay that they did that. Forgiveness is a way for you to release them from your life and your mind so that the memory of their harm cannot have power over you. You can forgive them in the privacy of your room by simply stating, "I forgive you." You don't have to say what for since you both know what it was, and you don't need to post it anywhere. Doing that is an open invitation to criticism, mockery, and just plain meanness that will be out there for everyone to see and either pity or hate you. And don't forgive someone until you are ready. It could take years, but I hope you will be able to work it out before time runs out. Start with forgiving yourself.

You are going to face times when apologizing to someone will mean the difference between having them remain in your life or not. If you were the one who messed up, you need to fix it. Throwing out a random "sorry" is not going to cut it. You want to make genuine eye contact, practice compassionate body language, and apologize with meaning. Don't let your ego rob you of a friendship. True friends are precious and so are parents. State what you did wrong, acknowledge your part, and explain what you intend to do to fix it so that it won't happen again. Actions always speak louder than words, so follow through.

Now, what if you need to forgive someone who has hurt you deeply? What if that hurt is so big, you can't ever imagine forgiving them? The mere thought of it makes you angry because you feel they deserve to have you mad at them for life. These are all fair and valid feelings, but here is what you might not know. This world is filled with people who may hurt you, intentionally or unintentionally— you may feel that they don't deserve your forgiveness. You may think that forgiving them means you are saying what they did was okay when it was not. You are not condoning what they did. Forgiving them is your ticket out of the prison of hate and anger that will destroy everything good about your life. Don't let them steal your joy. Forgive when you are ready to forgive. If you're not ready, just say so. Say it out loud, "I am not ready to forgive so-and-so yet." You don't have to forgive them in person. When you are ready, say their name and say, "I forgive you." Close the door on the memory and then forgive yourself.

CHAPTER 8:
HOW TO USE OPEN AND HONEST COMMUNICATION TO PARTNER WITH YOUR PARENTS FOR A HAPPIER LIFE

ADOLESCENTS/TEENS

Only some have the picture-perfect family you see portrayed in this picture. Even if they were real people and not actors, they would still have their failings, like all people do. They would have their struggles, like all families do.

Good communication is essential in a family unit. There are many kinds of families now, so you may be growing up in a way that is quite different from your parents' or grandparents' families. But, regardless of your family unit, effective communication can be a real peacekeeper. If you have one parent or two, a blended family, multicultural family members, or if you are living in a foster home, you will need effective communication skills. The quality of your life depends upon it. Communication takes work, and it may be harder in some families than others depending on your circumstances. It is much too big a subject to discuss at length in this book, but I will try to give you a basic foundation so you will have a starting place.

Some parents don't like to listen. Nobody listened to them when they were younger so they might not even know how to talk to you or work together to achieve a common goal, like getting along. You'll have to take this into consideration when you try to have a meaningful conversation with them. I am talking about a conversation that matters to both you and your parents and achieves something in the process. In other words, you both get something out of the deal.

First, get your thoughts together before you try to communicate with them. I recommend writing your thoughts down and keeping the notes with you. That way you won't forget the important things you want to discuss if the conversation temporarily veers off track. Parents nearly always get defensive when you tell them you would like to talk with them. You feel the same way when we do it to you, so the stage is set even before the conversation begins. Get those pre-judgments out of your head and stay in the moment. Focus on what is happening now. Stick to the plan.

Second, pick one or two things you need your parent's help with, the most urgent ones. It could be needing something to wear for a field trip or the Prom, or having to tell them that you lost your phone, got a "D" on a test, or that you want to take driving lessons. If you try to talk about too many things at once, it could turn into a one-sided, hit-and-run conversation with raised voices and insults. Nobody is going to win that one. You'll storm off without getting to say what you need to say, and it might be hard to start over again.

Next, always have a Plan B. In this case, Plan B might be to write your parents a letter, not a text but an actual letter. You can send it in an e-mail, but write it as a letter, keeping in mind that what you write will be written in stone in their minds. When you put some-thing in writing, think about something that someone will read more than once, maybe over and over. Don't EVER click Send on a first draft. Please print it out and put it in a safe, private place. You don't want your parents reading what you were thinking when your emotions were running high because that's what they'll remember. And we both know you didn't really mean it. Instead, let your letter sit for a day or two while your mind processes the emotions and feelings you have about what you are writing and who you are writ-ing it to. Read it out loud when you are reviewing it so you know how the words will sound when you say them. Then put it away. Take it back out and read it out loud again. If there is something you want to change, change it and put the letter away again. Take it out as often as you need to until you can say what you need in a plain, confident way. When you can read it without anger, self-doubt, or thinking you are just wasting your time anyway, it is ready to send.

We sometimes place adult expectations on your shoulders with no guidance on how to accomplish them. Then when you don't meet our expectations, we say things like, "Grow up; you aren't a kid an-ymore." It's not very fair, I know, and I won't make excuses for parents' behavior while demanding that you get it right the first time. It's an impossible goal and not very considerate, given that you are trying your best most of the time. These scenarios may make you start to ask yourself questions like, "Why can't I do anything right?" and "What's the point of trying?" or perhaps the worst one, "Why am I even here?"

Nobody wants to feel that way. It may seem like you have nowhere to turn, but have you given your parents a fair shot? There is a chance they don't know how you feel. As parents, we can drop the ball when it comes to figuring out what our teenagers need. We want you to be healthy and happy but if you don't tell us what you need, and we don't bother to ask, that's not good for anybody. Ask your parents to have a conversation with you and then explain the pressure you are feeling. If you feel awkward about a face-to-face conversation, then write them that letter or e-mail.

Be respectful and do your best to outline your feelings. Tell them if you're feeling overwhelmed and you haven't felt heard. Give them a chance to help.

If opening up to your parents is not an option, lean on a great friend, another family member, a teacher, or ask your parents about therapy. There are wonderful psychologists who specialize in working with young people. With most issues, you can talk it out, without the need for medication or radical treatments. Having an unbiased ear to listen to you is so very important in these situations. You want to feel heard. We all do. You matter. Don't judge yourself harshly because there are some problems you can't solve on your own. It is honorable and courageous to reach out and ask for help when you need it. However, always use caution when choosing a trusted source of help and comfort. If that little voice in your head or heart says something doesn't feel right, listen. If you are going to pour out your heart to someone, make sure it's the right someone.

PARENTS

Throughout most of their teen lives, parents haven't had to rely too much on two-way communication. When they were toddlers, we were busy teaching them to speak. As they progressed, we focused more on how they communicated with others, teaching them social skills like manners and the basics. We may not have noticed how challenging it is for them to have a regular conversation with us about something important to them. In some families, the only time parents talk to their kids is when we are angry. "How dare you speak to me that way!" "I am your father. Show me some respect when you talk to me."

Before it escalates to that level, have rational and calm conversations with your teens on a daily basis so that when you do communicate, you can do it in a respectful way. Surely there are more important and longer conversations to be had than an authoritative voice asking "Did you get your homework done?" or threatening "Don't be late, or you are grounded."

If you, on the other hand, are used to eye rolls, door slams, and the occasional, "Mom, I thought you said you would drive me to my friend's house," then you both need to work on respect, and that is a conversation on its own. Have a family meeting or sit down with your teen and discuss it. If you promised your teen something, keep your word, but don't allow them to disrespect you and then expect you to be there at their beck and call. It is a small respect to honor your word, but acts like these have a massive impact on your teen. Doing the right thing isn't always easy, but if you can do that most of the time, you will have demonstrated the importance of respect to your teen. They may criticize you or throw it up in your face later, but they will remember it, and one day, they will emulate your behavior.

When you sit down for a conversation, it shouldn't feel like a meeting at the principal's office. But it is a meeting, and meetings have an agenda, so write down what you want to get out of the meeting. Pick two things and ask your teen to pick two things. Write them down, and don't discuss anything else until you've covered those topics.

Set your expectations aside and think about your goal with this family communication. If your goal is to have calm, pleasant, and maybe even funny conversations with your teens, which is entirely attainable, then tell them that. Later, you will have to be more specific.

New strategies must be explored for the plan to work when your child is not a child anymore. You each have a role to play in the parent-teen partnership. You must recognize that your teens are on their way to adulthood, and you must keep that in mind and respect it when you communicate with them. What better way to teach your teen how to treat others with respect than to treat them with respect consistently? It will take practice, but you will have plenty of chances, so don't give up, okay?

How do we get them to open up? With time, patience, love, and acceptance, choosing your response with love—you will need all of these virtues. But don't worry; they will become habits and your communication techniques will serve you well throughout your life as long as you practice them regularly until they become a part of your inner rhythm. By this, I mean that once something becomes a habit, you don't have to think about every step anymore. You naturally do it, like walking, without thinking about every single action required in the process. You have heard of muscle memory. Well, this is something like that, and it works at the spiritual level as well as the physical level.

If your teen is having breakfast one morning and casually mentions that a friend was drinking at a party last night, and you explode into a diatribe about how you had better not catch your teen doing that, well, that conversation is pretty much over. Maybe your teen was going to ask a question or say something that would make you very proud, but you didn't wait to hear it. So now, you'll have to wait until the next time they try to communicate something important to you. After such an emotional reaction, trust dwindles, and anything you say usually only makes it worse.

If, however, your response is to ask if the friend made it home safe and if your teen has any feelings they want to share about it, you leave the conversation open. If your teen comes to you to confess something they have done, it can be tough not to overreact. But this is your time to show unconditional love, support, and understanding. For example, if your son sits down and tells you he tried vaping for the first time. He sees your face tighten up while you explode into a speech about lung cancer. You ground him and take away his screen privileges for a month. How likely do you think he will be to come to you with anything any time soon?

When something like this happens, there is a reason your teens come to you. They know what they did is unacceptable in your home, so take a deep breath, look them in the eye, and ask them, "Do you want to talk about it?" And let them talk. There might be silence at first. That's fine. They're thinking. They will talk if you wait. After they say their piece, you might say, "(NAME) you know how much I love you. I don't approve of what you did and there will be consequences, but right now, I'm just glad you're safe and that you came to me with this. Now get some rest and we'll talk more about this tomorrow".

I have found that asking the teen's input is very helpful in situations that require discipline. When you revisit the conversation the following day, at the end of the conversation, say something like, "I'd like for you to think about this and come up with something you think would be an appropriate punishment, okay?" I can almost guarantee they will come up with something much worse than what you would have doled out to them. Believe it or not, young people often have more honor than we give them credit for. Keeping your word and your promises means something to them. Don't back down. Honor whatever discipline you agree to and one appropriate to the offense.

Parents and teens can establish boundaries using respectful language and open communication. There is no reason for name-calling, yelling, or slamming doors. This behavior has to be modeled by you. If it rears its head from your teen, ignore it. If they demand a response in this heightened state, you merely tell them you can discuss things further when they have calmed down. It would be best if you modeled for them how adults handle these situations. They will mirror your behavior if you show them that this is how adults behave. We can show them, by example, how to regulate their emotions and handle situations calmly. Simply model the behavior you would like to see in your teen. It's never too early to start or too late.

Privacy
PARENTS
One big issue regarding respect is privacy. This goes for teens and adults. If the teen has his or her own room, knock before you enter when the door is closed. This is a common courtesy parents often ignore. Your teens aren't your babies anymore. It is still prudent to know their whereabouts whether they are at home or elsewhere. Of course, when friends are over and are congregating in the bedroom, it would not be inappropriate to ask your teen to leave the door slightly ajar.

Parents, when your teens are not at home, do not take the opportunity to search their rooms, unless it is literally a matter of life and death. If you have doubts or questions that you need to discuss with your teen, gently knock on the door and ask if you may come in. When you are in the room sit down near your teen in a place where you can both look each other in the eye. Ask them the question while you are both in their room. This is their domain and they will feel safe there.

By the same token, do not search their cell phone for messages and phone calls. If you trusted them enough to pay for a phone plan for them, then act like it. Again, if you have questions or are concerned about something specific, approach them when they are in their room and ask them about it. Then, wait for their answer.

And **TEENS**, do not look through your parent's checkbook or go into their bank or credit card accounts online, or purchase anything using their credit card without their permission. They should be talking to you about money in a constructive way. That is mentioned earlier in the book. You will need this information someday, but searching through your parents' private papers and other things is not appropriate. Such things can damage or destroy a person's credit and affect all aspects of their life, and yours. It is simply not worth the risk. If you have a question about money, ask it.

Work together to keep the communication lines open. We want our teens to be responsible for their own actions and behaviors. Obedience is necessary in times of potential danger, but as a rule, mutual respect and responsible behavior work just fine. We are all in this together.

Even though you don't need to go rummaging through their things like a crazy person, your teens are living under your roof so you do have a right to know what's going on in their lives. Take the time to discuss boundaries with your teens. Tell them what is important to you and why. Ask them the same question and listen closely to their answers. Establish boundaries that support good family communication.

Boundaries are important. Set boundaries with your teens and, once established, honor them. They will determine the "house rules" early on so your teen will know what is expected of him or her. Boundaries, along with unconditional love, respect, and forgiveness, will serve to build a strong family foundation, based on trust and honesty. No matter what changes may temporarily disrupt your peace, you will be able to work as a team to "get through anything". At no time should entitlement, threats, or disrespect by either of you be considered acceptable behavior. You are striving to create an environment that is conducive to raising a responsible, confident, productive, successful, and happy teenager. Together, you can achieve the outcome you both want and need. Believe me, it is so worth it.

For more information and suggestions for communicating with your teens, I recommend you visit Teen Brain Trust online at www.teenbraintrust.com. I think you will find it an excellent source of information that is helpful and easy to put into practice. Your teens and adolescents are on a grand adventure with many twists and turns. Some are as surprising and unexpected to them as they are to you. Their lives are dynamic and ever-changing in noticeable ways. It's our job as parents to keep up with those changes and to assess the quality of our family communication constantly. The Teen Prompts newsletter can help you do this in a way that will allow you to reinforce your support for your teens. And don't forget to check out the KidsHealth website. I think you will really like these resources.

Share the Transformative Power that
Essential Life Skills Can Have for Teens

You now know all the life skills that teens need to thrive, and the time has come to show other readers where they can find the same help.

Simply by leaving your honest opinion of this book on Amazon, you'll show other parents and teens that dynamic life principles like self-discipline, staying true to your mission, and a willingness to forgive are all part of personal fulfillment.

LET'S HEAR FROM YOU!
IF YOU ENJOYED THIS BOOK, PLEASE
LEAVE A REVIEW TO HELP OTHERS

Thank you for your help. You can encourage another teen to discover that being cool, emotionally balanced, and assertive are life skills that anybody can master if they put their mind to it.

https://www.amazon.com/review/create-review/?channel=glance-detail&asin=0966204956&ie=UTF8

CONCLUSION

You will learn many life skills as a teen that you will use throughout your life. I have outlined the basic skills which will serve as a foundation for many of the things you will learn later. Remember, the intention is not to overwhelm you with list upon list of more things to learn. This is meant to be a resource guide you can refer back to as often as you need to. It is broken down into basic life skills you should master before leaving your parent's home, followed by more in-depth life lessons that will serve you throughout your life.

There are also a number of Life Principles that determine how life works. If you practice them regularly, you will eventually be able to do them without even thinking. The intention is that they become second nature to you.

I have chosen the Five Dynamic Life Principles in Chapter 7 because you can use them any time you want to jumpstart your life and have more energy. Feel free to go back to them at any time for a refresher.

Life is dynamic, always changing. It doesn't stand still. Practicing these Five Dynamic Life Principles will help you adapt to the moment and the life situation. You can boost your energy, which will boost your life. The ability to be flexible and pivot as life changes will benefit you in many ways. It will ease your stress and anxiety as you move forward.

By using the Five Dynamic Life Principles outlined in this book, you will learn how to tap into your intuition and solve problems you previously thought were unsolvable.

This book will provide you with the tools you need to go beyond the limited scope of your mind and tap into a world of unlimited possibilities. Use some of the great tools to get back in touch with Nature. Try meditation to bring peace and balance. Be mindful of all your senses and how they can keep you centered and grateful.

Now that you know what to do, go out there and practice your new skills and the Five Dynamic Life Principles you just learned. It is okay if you don't get it right every time. You'll do great. You've got this; I believe in you.

I want to leave you with one last thought. As I mentioned earlier in this book, I struggled to maintain a relationship with my daughter for many years. I'm still working on it. I once asked her, "What if I can't change? How do we make this work?" Her advice was perfect, and I have let it guide me since then. She told me, "We don't give up on each other."

I want to leave you with that beautiful and loving piece of advice from my beloved daughter. Listen to each other. Communicate with each other. Love each other. Most importantly, don't give up on each other.

If you enjoyed the book, please tell a friend and leave a review on Amazon. Thank you!

ABOUT THE AUTHOR

Bernadette Greggory is an author, a Holistic Wellness Consultant, and an avid aviation enthusiast. She was raised in the Midwestern United States and is one of twelve children. She has one daughter.

Bernadette is a personal empowerment trainer and has taught parenting and child development classes on self-esteem, effective communication, and leadership skills, among others. She was also a medical radio talk show host and has been a writer for many years.

She believes that many young people are being short-changed in today's fast-paced techno environment. "Opportunities for independent thinking seem to be slipping away as many parents are not always able or willing to "be there" for their adolescents and teens. This leaves it to schools, social media, and other outside influences to act as teachers and support systems at a most critical time in their growth and development. Information and resources that once guided and supported families have become obsolete in today's society. More information is needed if the journey from childhood to adulthood is to be a successful one."

Bernadette has always been an adventurer who believes life is the greatest adventure of all. She wrote this book because of the difference she believes the information it contains can make in the lives of teens and parents as they make this journey together.

Bernadette also believes nothing is more important than preparing young people for life beyond survival mode, where they can find peace of heart and true happiness.

GLOSSARY

Adolescence: The process of growing up. The period of life from ages 10 to 19, during which a child develops into an adult.

Amygdala: An almond-shaped piece of the brain located in the temporal lobe and primarily associated with emotional processes.

Anxiety: A feeling of dread or apprehension in apparently harmless situations when no actual danger is present. It isn't the same as fear which occurs when someone is clearly in real danger, such as in the case of a physical threat or attack. Anxiety is common when you do not feel completely in control, such as taking a test you may not be prepared for, speaking in front of a group, or going out on a blind date.

Cerebellum: The part of the brain that is responsible for balancing the coordination of your muscles and your equilibrium.

Collaborate: To work together with others for a common goal or a desired outcome. This happens in school but will occur often in work situations as well.

Connection: An invisible link between a person and one's self, another person, Nature, God or the Universe; an inner bond that is strong and deep, and is usually mutual, but not necessarily romantic. Like-minded people who share the same interests or beliefs often have a connection with each other.

Debilitating: Something that weakens you.

Demographic: The statistical characteristics of our population, e.g., age or income.

Depression: A mood or emotional state usually accompanied by feelings of guilt or worthlessness. It can make you feel pessimistic, lethargic, and isolated. Drastic life changes like the loss of a loved one or pet, your parents getting a divorce, your best friend moving away, or even not getting enough sleep can cause temporary depression. If it goes on for a long time, depression can affect the chemical balance in your body and medication may be needed to snap you out of it. Sometimes, depression can make you feel so hopeless that you feel like ending your life. If you have thoughts of suicide, get help immediately.

Discriminate: To recognize distinctions between one thing and another. Used in its negative sense, discrimination refers to any time we unjustly judge a person based on certain distinctions such as race, age, sex, disability, or sexual orientation. This can be a case of you choosing one of your close friends to work in your group instead of the new kid in class or disrespecting someone because they belong to another culture, race, or religion that you disapprove of.

Divinity: Refers to the quality or state of being God-like.

Doctrine: Something a particular group believes in that is often strict and sometimes limited in its view. This could be a Church, political party, or another group whose ideas might be the same or different from yours.

Dynamic: Energetic force that stimulates constant change, activity, or progress; life is always changing and, therefore, is dynamic.

Empathy: This is when you care about and are sensitive to what another is feeling or what they are experiencing.

Entrepreneur: Someone who decides to take responsibility for starting and running their own business rather than working for someone else. There is more risk and responsibility, but many young people enjoy successful careers as entrepreneurs.

Forgiveness: Forgiveness means different things to different people. Generally, however, it involves a conscious decision to let go of anger and resentment from a past hurt so you can be free to move on with your life.

Grey Matter: Holds the majority of the neuronal cell bodies and creates regions of the brain that are vital for self-control, decision-making, sensory perception, and muscle coordination.

Hormones: Chemicals that coordinate different bodily functions by carrying messages through your blood to your organs, skin, muscles, and other tissues. Scientists have identified over 50 hormones in the human body so far. Hormones control many bodily processes, including metabolism, homeostasis (constant internal balance), blood pressure, blood sugar regulation, fluid (water) and electrolyte balance, body temperature, growth and development, sexual function, reproduction, the sleep-wake cycle, and mood.

Integrity: Adherence to a code of moral, artistic, or other values.

Intuition: The power of knowing immediately and without conscious reasoning; an inner nudge, a gut feeling, or a hunch beyond what your logical mind tells you. Tuition, or outer knowledge, says, "I think, therefore I am." Intuition, or inner knowledge, says, "How do you know you think?

Meditation: According to the Cleveland Clinic, "meditation is a practice that involves focusing or clearing your mind using a combination of mental and physical techniques". Meditation is often used to calm the mind in order to achieve a greater inner awareness and clarity, and to reduce stress. Music, incense, the stillness of Nature, and chanting a sacred word are among the techniques used in meditation. Tai Chi, an internal Chinese martial art, is also considered a form of meditation.

Mindfulness: Attempting to hold a non-judgmental space for your thoughts and emotions.

Perspective: A point of view; an attitude; the way you interpret what is going on around you in the world at any given moment.

Pivot: A person, thing, or factor having a central role or effect.

Principle: A comprehensive and fundamental law, doctrine, or assumption; a rule or code of conduct.

Priorities: A list of tasks arranged in order of importance; the things that are most important to you and need your attention first. These change when a task is completed or an emergency interrupts the ordered series of tasks competing for your attention.

GLOSSARY | 133

Self-Confidence: This is the confidence you have in yourself with regard to your abilities.

Self-Esteem: A self-concept of your value as a person and the satisfaction you feel in being who you are; how you regard yourself.

Social Sensitivity: This refers to your own ability to understand, perceive, and respect the feelings and viewpoints of others.

References: These will be important when you are preparing for a job interview. They are people who can speak on behalf of your character. Often, these can be teachers, former bosses, or places where you have volunteered.

REFERENCES

Alexander, K. L. (2019). *Biography: Toni Morrison.* Womens History. https://www.womenshistory.org/education-resources/biographies/toni-morrison#:~:text=Toni%20Morrison%20is%20one%20of

Bannister, S. (2021). *There is no Wifi in the forest.* Health Is Always Available. https://sharonbannister.uk/there-is-no-wifi-in-the-forest-but-i-promise-you-will-have-a-better-connection/#:~:text=There%20is%20no%20WIFI%20in,a%20better%20connection%20%2D%20Sharon%20Bannister

Booth, M. Z., & Gerard, J. M. (2011). Self-esteem and academic achievement: A comparative study of adolescent students in England and the United States. *Compare: A Journal of Comparative and International Education, 41*(5), 629–648. https://doi.org/10.1080/03057925.2011.566688

Carroll, J. E., Gruenewald, T. L., Taylor, S. E., Janicki-Deverts, D., Matthews, K. A., & Seeman, T. E. (2013). *Childhood abuse, parental warmth, and adult multisystem biological risk in the coronary artery risk development in young adults study.* Proceedings of the National Academy of Sciences, 110(42), 17149–17153. https://doi.org/10.1073/pnas.1315458110

Dewar, G. (2020, August 22). *Teaching empathy: Evidence-based tips for fostering empathic awareness in children.* PARENTING SCIENCE. https://parentingscience.com/teaching-empathy-tips/

Khan, S. A. (2020, September 18). *Examples of showing respect to others & why it's important?* Legacy Business Cultures. https://legacycultures.com/examples-of-showing-respect-to-others-and-its-importance-in-life/

Kramer, S. (2009, November 26). *Problem solving with a relaxation meditation for teens.* Integral Yoga Magazine. https://integralyogamagazine.org/problem-solving-with-a-relaxation-meditation-for-teens/

Louise, E. (2013, September 6). *Coaching tools 101: The urgent important matrix - what it is and how to use it!* | the launchpad - the coaching tools company blog. The Coaching Tools Company. https://www.thecoachingtoolscompany.com/coaching-tools-101-what-is-the-urgent-important-matrix/

Mackinson, R. (2021, October 7). *Elon musk: The inspirational success story of Tesla's CEO.* CEO Today. https://www.ceotodaymagazine.com/2021/10/elon-musk-the-inspirational-success-story-of-teslas-ceo/#:~:text=From%20a%20young%20age%2C%20Musk

Maddy. (2020, August 16). *The heartbreaking but inspiring success story of Oprah Winfrey.* WISURU. https://wisuru.com/biography/the-success-story-of-oprah-winfrey/#:~:text=Looking%20at%20this%2C%20her%20grandmother

Maselko, J., Kubzansky, L., Lipsitt, L., & Buka, S. L. (2010). *Mother's affection at 8 months predicts emotional distress in adulthood.* Journal of Epidemiology & Community Health, 65(7), 621–625. https://doi.org/10.1136/jech.2009.097873

MD, C. M. (2022, January 25). *5 skills teens need in life — and how to encourage them.* Harvard Health. https://www.health.harvard.edu/blog/5-skills-teens-need-in-life-and-how-to-encourage-them-202201252674

Merriam Webster. (n.d.). *Intuition.* In Merriam-Webster.com dictionary. Retrieved October 18, 2022, from https://www.merriam-webster.com/dictionary/intuition?utm_campaign=sd&utm_medium=serp&utm_source=jsonld

MindTools. (2016). *SMART goals – how to make your goals achievable.* Mindtools; Emerald Works. https://www.mindtools.com/pages/article/smart-goals.htm

Monroe, J. (2018, April 16). *How nature supports teen mental health.* Newport Academy. https://www.newportacademy.com/resources/mental-health/how-nature-supports-teen-mental-health/

Moriarty, D. (2020, January 16). *How to say sorry and mean it—your teen mag.* Your Teen Magazine. https://yourteenmag.com/family-life/communication/how-to-say-sorry

NewFolks. (2020, October 13). *How to teach teens to respect you as a parent.* NewFolks. https://www.newfolks.com/stages/teach-teens-to-respect-parents/

Nixon, C. (2016). *What adolescents (or teenagers) need to thrive* [Video]. YouTube. https://www.youtube.com/watch?v=S05PBOIdSeE

Quote Fancy. (n.d.). *Top 50 Richard Stallam quotes.* https://quotefancy.com/quote/1425630/Richard-Stallman-Sharing-knowledge-is-the-most-fundamental-act-of-friendship-Because-it

REACHOUT. (2019). *Self-esteem and teenagers - reachout parents.* Reachout. https://parents.au.reachout.com/common-concerns/everyday-issues/self-esteem-and-teenagers

REACHOUT. (2022). *Help your teenager build positive self-esteem - reachout parents*. Parents.au.reachout. https://parents.au.reachout.com/common-concerns/everyday-issues/things-to-try-self-esteem/help-your-teenager-build-positive-self-esteem

Reed, S. (2022, March 18). *15 inspiring parenting quotes to live by*. Care. https://www.care.com/c/inspirational-parenting-quotes/#:~:text=%E2%80%9CIt%20is%20not%20what%20you

Roser, M., Ortiz-Ospina, E., & Ritchie, H. (2013). *World Population Growth*. Our World in Data. https://ourworldindata.org/world-population-growth

The Parenting Network. (2022). *Talking with teens – the importance of open communication*. Masandpas. https://masandpas.com/talking-with-teens-how-important-is-it-to-keep-the-communication-channels-open/

Yousafzai, M. (2022). *Malala's story*. Malala Fund. https://malala.org/malalas-story

Made in the USA
Monee, IL
11 June 2023

35539022R00079